The Seven Natural
Laws of Love

By Deborah Taj Anapol, Ph.D.

Elite Books
Santa Rosa, CA 95403
www.Elitebooks.biz

Library of Congress Cataloging-in-Publication Data:

Anapol, Deborah M.

    The seven natural laws of love / by Deborah Anapol.—1st ed.

    p. cm.

    Includes bibliographical references.

    ISBN 0-9710888-7-X

    1. Love. I. Title.

BD436.A53 2005

128'.46—dc22

2005009793

Cover by Vicki Valentine
Interior by Nan Sea Love
Typeset in Eva and Hoefler Text
Printed in USA
First Edition
10 9 8 7 6 5 4 3 2 1

CONTENTS

INTRODUCTION

We imagine that we need to be loved and recognized as a totally unique being, as an entity separate from the common mortal by our greatness, and this also is a distorted translation of an essential need, the need to be recognized as non-separate from the world, as a stream of love independent of an elevated ego. — DANIEL ODIER, Desire

We speak of love as if we know what it is and where it comes from when the truth is that for most of us, love is a mystery. At the same time, there is nothing we want more. As the Beatles sang, "All we need is love. Love is all we need."

This universal longing for love leads us to search for someone or something that will satisfy our hunger. The problem is that most of us don't fully understand what it is we're seeking. No wonder our experiences of love so often prove to be transitory and elusive!

Like many people, I've spent much of my life in pursuit of true love. I even made a career of it. Over the years I explored many different kinds of intimate relationships and many different spiritual paths and practices. On occasion I tasted love that was deeply nourishing, yet something was still missing, and I didn't know what it was. The inner restlessness that first started me on this quest would not be satisfied until I'd gotten to the bottom of this mystery called love.

As a therapist, seminar leader, and relationship coach, I've watched clients encountering the same dead ends, blind alleys, and misperceptions over and over as they sought to find love with each other. I've made the same mistakes myself, not once, but many times as I tried one strategy after another to find the love I so desired.

We tell ourselves, "If only I can find the right partner, or get the partner I have to give me what I want, or make myself or my partner be different in some way, then I will feel loved." Even though I knew better, it was a long, long time before I stopped trying to find love outside myself.

After working with thousands of people who are love-sick, love-starved, or love-intoxicated, I have to conclude that most people are just as confused as I was about how this powerful force called love operates. We've been taught that love is one thing, but the reality is that what we believe love to be has little to do with genuine love. We've fallen for a Disneyland version of love that effectively distracts us from discovering the real thing.

This book invites you to let go of the idea that love is a means to an end. Instead of seeing love as something that will make you happy if you can get enough of it, consider the possibility of love as way of being, of love as a state of consciousness. As such it is independent of any particular person or set of conditions. In other words, love is unlimited, impersonal and unchanging. It cannot be lost nor can it be hoarded. This kind of love is both a choice and a surrender to something beyond your ego.

A romantic epiphany can catalyze a deeper exploration of love, as it did for me, but the fantasy of finding completion in another human being inevitably leads us astray if we refuse to grow beyond this stage. Love is by nature completely unselfish. When people come together in an open and defenseless way with no agenda, love can be shared. Any desire to find in the other a solution to your needs, or an escape from confronting your own sense of separation, your own fears and anxieties, translates into attachment, dependency, and manipulation, not love.

Genuine love is an energy that arises when your sense of identity expands beyond the individual self. Love leads to an awareness of union with something larger than yourself. Call it the Divine, call it the Absolute, call it Existence, or the Universe, call it whatever you want, but know that ultimately, nothing less will satisfy the heartfelt longing for love. From this perspective, you do not deserve love, you *are* love. This kind of love is contagious—when you come into contact with someone who carries this energy, it sparks that awareness in you.

I remember sitting by a stream in a beautiful wooded valley over twenty years ago trying to recover my composure after a highly emotional dispute with my husband. The issue we were struggling with was one which popped up again and again without ever finding permanent resolution and I felt hopeless about our future. As I sat there contemplating what to do, the words came to me, "We have to become more conscious."

Before I had a chance to even wonder what this meant, I noticed that the sound of the water flowing through the streambed had become very loud. The light filtering through the trees suddenly grew almost blindingly bright and the rocks in the stream glittered with dazzling sunbeams. The trees began to glow and I could feel the movement of sap and the exchange of oxygen and carbon dioxide taking place. I had the peculiar sensation that I *was* one of the trees, with roots reaching deep into the earth.

Suddenly I felt a strange and wonderful shift in perspective. I was no longer a woman sitting on a patch of dirt, full of troubled thoughts. I was the stream, and the rocks, and the earth, and the trees. I was all of it and none of it. I sat there for some unknown amount of time until an increasing chill in the air brought me back to myself.

The argument that had seemed so important a few minutes ago now seemed insignificant. The frustration that had felt so oppressive was replaced with a deep inner peace and joy. Slowly I got up and walked back to my husband and our friends and tried to communicate what I'd experienced. They didn't entirely understand what I was saying, but they did feel the change in my energy and love prevailed for a time.

This experience changed me forever, but I still had much to learn about how love moves in the world. This book is a distillation of all I have discovered in over thirty years of messy first hand experience and intensive psychological and spiritual study.

The first law of love, namely that love is its own law, is the basis for all the rest. It helps us to know the difference between "laws" that are in harmony with nature, and those that are not. We imagine that love follows dozens of laws invented by men and women, when the truth is that love is not subject to man-made codes or societal customs.

Rather, love is governed by a small number of universal laws. These laws can be found at the heart of all spiritual teachings. They are not specific to love. In fact, people often want to take exception to these laws when it comes to love, because to apply spiritual law to human love challenges many beliefs and assumptions.

These "laws" of love are not commandments. They aren't laws in the sense of being a written code of behavior, with prescribed punishments for breaking each one. We could instead call them principles, or characteristics, or qualities. I use the word *law* to suggest that it makes no difference whether you know these laws or agree with them. Their power is unaffected. In this sense, the seven natural laws of love are more real than any man-made law.

I did not invent the seven natural laws of love. I simply discovered that they govern the movement of love in the world just as surely as the laws of physics govern the interactions of matter and energy. Not because some authority says so, but because this is how things work. Our knowledge of physics grows as we make new discoveries. As our knowledge of physics becomes more refined, we find that it corresponds more and more closely to ancient spiritual teachings about the nature of reality. And so it is with love.

Don't take my word for it. Instead, I invite you to explore with me whether these seven laws *do* apply to love! If what I say doesn't seem to fit your own experience, investigate for yourself. My intention is not to create yet another system of fixed beliefs, but to open the gateway to allowing more love to be felt in this world.

Chapter One
Love Is Its Own Law

*If there are any morals or principles they all arise from love, for that is the only principle
and moral which is real. There are many doctrines and principles made by man, but these are simply
laws; love has its own law and it adheres to the law of no one.*
—*HAZRAT INAYAT KHAN,* The Sufi Message

Love is a force of nature. However much we may want to, we can not command, demand, or disappear love, any more than we can command the moon and the stars and the wind and the rain to come and go according to our whims. We may have some limited ability to change the weather, but we do so at the risk of upsetting an ecological balance we don't fully understand. Similarly, we can stage a seduction or mount a courtship, but the result is more likely to be infatuation, or two illusions dancing together, than love.

Love is bigger than you are. You can invite love, but you cannot dictate how, when, and where love expresses itself. You can choose to surrender to love, or not, but in the end love strikes like lightning— unpredictable and irrefutable. You can even find yourself loving people you don't like at all. Love does not come with conditions, stipulations, addendums, or codes. Like the sun, love radiates independently of our fears and desires.

Love is inherently free. It cannot be bought, sold, or traded. You cannot make someone love you, nor can you prevent it, for any amount of money. Love cannot be imprisoned nor can it be legislated. Love is not a substance, not a commodity, nor even a marketable power source. Love has no territory, no borders, no quantifiable mass or energy output.

One can buy sex partners and even marriage partners. Marriage is a matter for the law, for rules and courts and property rights. In the past, the marriage price, or dowry, and in the present, alimony, and the pre-nuptial agreement, make it clear that marriage is all about contracts. But as we all know, marriages, whether arranged or not, may have little to do with love.

Sexual stimulation and gratification, whether by way of fingers, mouths, objects, fantasy play, whips and chains, or just plain intercourse, can certainly be bought and sold, not to mention used to sell other things. Whether sex should be for sale is another question entirely, but love itself can not be sold.

One can buy loyalty, companionship, attention, perhaps even compassion, but love itself cannot be bought. An orgasm can be bought, but love cannot. It comes, or not, by grace, of its own will and in its own timing, subject to no human's planning.

Love cannot be turned on as a reward. It cannot be turned off as a punishment. Only something else pretending to be love can be used as a lure, as a hook, for bait and switch, imitated, insinuated, but the real deal can never be delivered if it doesn't spring freely from the heart.

This doesn't mean that love allows destructive and abusive behaviors to go unchecked. Love speaks out for justice and protests when harm is being done. Love points out the consequences of hurting oneself or others. Love allows room for anger, grief, or pain to be expressed and released. But love does not threaten to withhold itself if it doesn't get what it wants. Love does not say, directly or indirectly, "If you are a bad boy, Mommy won't love you any more." Love does not say, "Daddy's little girl doesn't do that." Love does not say, "If you want to be loved you must be nice, or do what I want, or never love anyone else, or promise you'll never leave me."

Love cares what becomes of you because love knows that we are all interconnected. Love is inherently compassionate and empathic. Love knows that the "other" is also oneself. This is the true nature of love and love itself can not be manipulated or restrained. Love honors the sovereignty of each soul. Love is its own law.

Love and Expectations

Most of us are quite sure that we know exactly how others should treat us, and how we should treat others, especially those with whom we share a bond of love. When your expectations about what a beloved should do are not met, you might respond with hurt, anger, and blame. When you don't behave the way you think you should, you're likely to feel guilt or shame.

Perhaps you've attempted to avoid these reactions by trying not to have expectations, but usually this just compounds the problem by burying your unmet expectations—and your resentment—deeper. You are only deceiving yourself. Perhaps you've tried to avoid making judgments, but again, what usually happens is that the judgments go into hiding, making them even harder to release.

We would do far better to realize that love has its own laws to which it always adheres, but these are not the laws we have been taught. Arguing with love's own laws does no good at all. Understanding the true nature of love enhances our lives.

We have all absorbed beliefs about love, and about morality, as children. Usually these beliefs come from our parents. They don't have to be spoken out loud, although sometimes they are. We may also take on beliefs, consciously or unconsciously, from church, school, movies, songs, books, television, friends, neighbors, or other family members. Unfortunately, most of these sources also have a distorted understanding of love and loving relationships.

When I was a young woman, Tolstoy's classic love story, *Anna Karenina,* made a big impression on me. I had read the novel as a young teenager, but it wasn't until I watched the serialized television version on PBS in my late twenties that I consciously heard its emotion-laden message. Thankfully, I noticed that the conflict Anna felt between her duty to her husband and attachment to her young son, and the erotic love she experienced with her dashing young lover, is only resolved when she throws herself in the path of a speeding train!

I quickly decided that the moral of this story of separation between love, desire, and responsibility—and the punishment of passionate women—was not the kind of programming I wanted! Tolstoy's novel reflects the belief that love necessitates pain. This idea was very popular in the nineteenth century, and even today it continues to influence us, but it's not congruent with natural law. The misinformation that we take for truth may have been passed down for generations, but that doesn't change the fact that it is untrue. So how are we to know the difference between man-made laws and those that arise from love?

Natural Law

The laws of nature can be known through our observations of the natural world. They are simply descriptions of how elements, energies, and life forms interact. The laws of physics arise from man's attempts to understand and specify how these natural laws operate. For example, gravity is a natural force which impacts all matter. We are subject to the laws of gravity whether or not we believe in gravity. If you jump off a cliff you will fall to the ground, even if you believe you can fly, unless you are using a device such as a hang glider. And you will fall at a rate that can be predetermined if certain parameters are known.

If water is heated to two hundred and twelve degrees Fahrenheit it will boil. If you want to boil water, the water must be put in a watertight container which can withstand being heated to this temperature. It simply will not work to pour the water over the fire, or to use a plastic container, or to put the pot of water under the fire instead of over the fire. It makes no difference what day of the week it is or that you believe the fire will cool the water instead of heat it. If you are at a high altitude, it will take longer for the water to boil than it will take at sea level. Nevertheless, given enough fire and enough water in the right relationship, the water will boil.

Death is another good example of a natural law. The wheel of life goes round and round as the old gives way to the new. We cannot have creation without destruction. If an animal is prevented from breathing or if food and water are withheld for a period of time, the body will become lifeless and begin to decay. If the vital organs of the body stop functioning, or if sufficient blood is lost, the body dies. There may be some variation in how long different bodies can remain alive under adverse conditions, but death of the body is inevitable when life essentials are unavailable.

Sometimes our observations mislead us. Those who have been near death and returned to tell us about it report that their consciousness seemed to exist independently of the body. These near death experiences suggest that "death" is merely a transition into some other realm. We identify with our bodies, but there is at least some evidence that we have a mysterious existence apart from the body. Be this as it may, we know that the body can die.

In the past, many people believed that the earth was flat and that the sun revolved around the earth. It looked that way, they'd always been told it was that way, and when evidence to the contrary appeared the Vatican suppressed it vigorously. Nevertheless, we've now altered our beliefs to incorporate new information. Despite appearances, it's now agreed that the earth is round and it orbits our sun.

Modern physics tells us that all matter is mostly space, but it looks solid to us. Science has also discovered that all matter is vibrating, even though it doesn't look that way to the naked eye. Yet, most people have grown up believing that matter is solid and inanimate and so they keep seeing and feeling matter as solid, even though the data says it's not.

We make the same mistakes about the laws of love. We create conditions which are not very likely to attract or sustain love because that's what we've been taught to do. We confuse love with its counterfeits. Sometimes we don't even know how to recognize the real thing when we see it. Then we wonder where love has gone. We do the equivalent of trying to boil water in a plastic pot and can't understand why the result is a messy meltdown.

Man-made Laws

Many people believe that when a person says, "I love you," this is proof of love. Conversely, when these magic words are not spoken, it is taken to mean that love is not present. But this is a man-made law, not a natural one. How many people routinely mouth the words because they're told it's appropriate, or they want something in return, or they know it's expected? Others deliberately withhold the words because they're afraid of creating expectations or have a story that love is too sacred to speak of, or think saying "I love you" is a promise to behave in a certain way.

Recently a man who I'd been involved with a few years ago phoned me to tell me he wanted to communicate some things he'd been unaware of when were together. He went on to describe our last sexual encounter appreciatively, saying that he'd never experienced anything so powerful. He went on to say he'd been deeply disturbed that we hadn't exchanged "I love you's" before, during, or after this ecstatic time together.

He believed that declarations of love were supposed to be part of passionate lovemaking. In the absence of this verbal communication from me, he doubted that I loved him. He was only vaguely conscious of the hurt and anger that arose in him as a result, so he was unable to communicate with me about it. Instead he found himself reacting by distancing from me and putting his attention on other women. I was confused by his behavior and felt abandoned. How could he behave this way after the powerful connection we had shared? I was clueless, never suspecting he was reacting to my perceived verbal withholding. Instead I concluded that he didn't value our relationship and withdrew myself.

Several years later as I listened to his story I felt tremendous sadness. This man-made law could be stated:

If the words "I love you" are not spoken, love is not present.

This belief had caused much mischief. While we may well have ended up parting ways, there was no need for either of us to part feeling unloved by the other.

Perhaps you too have experienced a misunderstanding like this one. Many people I've worked with have felt immense grief when they realize how much they longed to have a parent say, "I love you." They may have spent years feeling unloved before finally hearing these words, sometimes from the deathbed. Then they realize the love was always there but was never expressed in words. Similarly, when a loved one dies before we speak our love to them, the grief is often doubled.

Sandra and Ralph had been friends and colleagues for half a dozen years when Ralph suddenly had a stroke and died without regaining consciousness. Sandra's disturbance over Ralph's swift passing was unexpectedly profound—and suppressed at the same time. She found it impossible to openly mourn his death, but was aware of intense grief which seemed out of proportion to their friendship. As we explored her feelings, she became aware that in the wake of a dispute with Ralph, she had withdrawn her gratitude and admiration for him. The dispute had been resolved, but she had never fully opened her heart again and told him how much she valued him. His untimely death left Sandra sitting with dammed up affection.

Conversely, sometimes people have the experience of hearing the words "I love you" but inwardly feeling the words are a lie. Instead of trusting the gut feeling, they believe they should feel loved. They may judge themselves for not being open to the love or decide that they are damaged and unable to tolerate being loved. If they later learn their intuition was accurate, they may go on to become mistrustful of others and doubt that the words and the love could ever be congruent.

You may feel a need for reassurance when you rightly sense a person is closed to love. Often, the discrepancy between words and other channels of expression does indicate some unhealed wounds which can create discomfort and confusion all around.

A woman I'll call Marilyn was puzzled by her experience with her boyfriend Gary. "I'm just crazy about Gary," she told me. "He's super-attentive, spends every weekend with me, calls often, and is planning fabulous vacations with me. We always have a great time together and he's a wonderful lover, but he never says, 'I love you' so I don't either. What should I do?"

As I learned more about Marilyn and Gary, I discovered that Gary's wife had committed suicide some years before. His grief and shock was so great that he'd unconsciously made a decision never to open his heart again. He very much enjoyed his time with Marilyn, but he was determined not to allow love in. Love was knocking at the door of his closed heart, but he was doing his best to resist it. When Marilyn reflected on Gary's history, she decided to give Gary more time to heal and slowly let love in again before jumping to any conclusions about their future.

There is nothing wrong with saying, "I love you," and there is nothing wrong with longing to hear it spoken. Just know that you are assuming a connection between the words and the love itself that may be there only in your imagination. This is just one of many man-made laws. Unlike natural law which always holds true, the man-made "laws" of love have no basis in reality. They are merely beliefs, but we take them very seriously. If we knew the difference between natural laws and man-made laws of love our lives would be much happier!

EXERCISE:

Make your own list of the "laws" of love that influence your behavior and perceptions. Be honest, and don't try to make yourself look good. Give at least ten assumptions or beliefs you have about love, even if you suspect their authenticity.

In the film *Bliss,* newlyweds play a game they call *If You Really Loved Me.* Each takes a turn completing the sentence, "If you really loved me you would...." This format could be a good way to construct your list if you're having trouble uncovering your hidden operating instructions. When your list is complete, ask yourself these questions about each item:

Where did I acquire this belief? Does it enhance the quality of my life and relationships? Can I know that it's true? (Hint: There is no such thing as a belief that is true. By its very nature, a belief is *believed,* rather than a fact which can be known unequivocally.)

Love and Morality

Many people seem to think that sex and morality are the same thing, but really it is love and morality that are directly related. If we are confused about what constitutes love in the personal arena we will also be confused about what constitutes morality in the world at large. If people were taught to honor the true nature of love in every aspect of life, we wouldn't need books full of complicated and detailed laws—or legions of lawyers and judges to interpret them.

When spiritual teacher Hazrat Inayat Khan,[1] who brought the ancient teachings of Sufism to America in the 1920s, says that love is the only moral which is real, he is pointing to the essential unity of love and morality. Morality is love in action. Any law that isn't based on love is likely to be unjust.

Have you ever noticed that when you're really, really angry with someone, you don't want to tell them what they've done to offend you? In fact, you may not want to communicate with them at all, especially if you don't have much invested in the relationship. You probably have thoughts about what a miserable, rotten, disgusting human being so-and-so is, and if you're mad enough you might fantasize their imminent and painful death. Or you might feel that death would be too kind a punishment and wish them far worse. You might want to strip them of their most valued possessions, or wish to humiliate and discredit them.

Or perhaps you just want to send them away somewhere you'll never have to see them again, and make sure there is no way they can repeat their offense.

All of these impulses and desires are common ways that humans respond when they lose touch with the love inside and out. There is nothing wrong with having these feelings. It's perfectly human to get angry. It happens to us all to a greater or lesser extent, but anger is a strange foundation for the law of the land. Yet this kind of thinking is precisely the basis for both our criminal and civil justice systems. When someone is convicted of a crime, they may be fined, imprisoned, or put to death. They may lose respect, their livelihood, or their right to travel or live in certain places.

Some people feel that there is no good reason to apply spiritual principles to criminal justice. After all, isn't separation of church and state the law of the land? But we are not talking about any particular church or faith, we are talking about whether the laws of our land should be based on love or hate. In any case, scientific research offers much data in support of the premise that punishment is less effective than reward in shaping behavior.

The evidence is also clear that modeling is the most powerful of all learning modalities. The Law of Attraction (Chapter Three) explains why this is so. If we want people to behave in a more considerate, compassionate way, we need to treat them with compassion and consideration. "Do what I say and not what I do" just doesn't work. If what we want is an effective way to end crime, we would make choices in harmony with natural law. Our response to problematic behaviors would certainly include natural consequences which might be unpleasant, but the response would not stem from anger or the desire for revenge.

There is an old saying that love is blind, but it would be more accurate to say that hate is blind. Love sees clearly what is needed to bring a person or situation into balance and freely offers whatever it can toward that end.

Chapter Two
The Law of Source

That which is mysteriously evoked in the presence of some being, this great love, can never be lost.
You can only imagine it to be lost if you imagine it to be located someplace other than where you are.
—GANGAJI

The second law of love is *You Are the Source of Love.* You! Not your husband or your wife, not your lover, not your parents, not your guru, not your child, not your dog or cat, not anyone but you. Love is within each of us and radiates outward. If you really knew the truth of this law, your whole reality would change instantaneously.

All of the time and energy spent anxiously seeking love and approval from others would be immediately liberated for more creative pursuits. All of the misery generated by disappointment about not being loved by family, friends, or romantic partners would fade into oblivion. The struggle to find love and keep love would be transformed into the pleasure of lavishing love on others. The battle to avoid or deny the perceived emptiness inside would be over. The fear of not being loved and all the stories about not deserving love would dissolve, leaving peace and contentment in their wake.

Imagine for a moment that you know beyond a shadow of a doubt that your very nature is pure love. Imagine that you can make a choice at any moment simply to love, without any cause, without any target, without any conditions. Imagine this is known to you through your own direct experience, not as a theory, not as wishful thinking. The very idea may sound intolerably corny to you, but just for the moment, put aside any cynical thoughts you may be having and see if you can make contact with the love that you are.

A sacred text from India, *The Changogya Upanishad*[2] puts it this way:

> *"As vast as this space without is the tiny space within your heart: heaven and earth are found in it,*
> *fire and air, sun and moon, lightening and the constellations, whatever belongs to you here below*
> *and all that doesn't, all this is gathered in that tiny space within your heart."*

EXERCISE:

Deep inside you, in the very core of your being, in the innermost chamber of your heart, is an everlasting reservoir of love. This is the well that never runs dry, the secret lamp that never runs out of oil. Its flame glows steadily no matter what happens. If you put your complete attention on this inner flame of love, you will be filled with a sense of peace, well being, and total acceptance. Remember that your true nature is love. Place your awareness on your own center point and allow the love to flow, to fill you to overflowing.

Are you able to sense this presence? Do you feel the truth of this possibility that love resides in your own heart? Stop reading for a minute and see if you can experience this reality for yourself. What happens inside when you remind yourself that your whole being is nothing but love? What happens inside when you decide to love for no reason? If you're not there yet, don't worry. Years and years of brainwashing may take a little time and energy to undo. Try it again as you finish each chapter of this book.

The Great Mistake

When the infant's caretakers do not embody the knowledge that they are their own source of love, but instead believe that love comes from outside, in the sphere of their influence, the baby soon forgets that his or her very essence is love. So many of us were not born into loving environments or were later surrounded by people who were disconnected from their own inner source, it's not surprising we have difficulty realizing the source is not outside ourselves.

When a child is taught to seek love from others and to make herself conform to their desires in order to earn or keep this love, she learns to abandon her own intuitive knowing. Before long the child becomes desperate to find and keep loving contact with others. Just as we need food and water to survive, as infants our very survival depends upon receiving affection and nurturing touch.

If we do not receive a bare minimum of loving contact, in addition to food and shelter, the absence of tender touch can be life-threatening. Health care professionals first observed this phenomenon in orphanages where babies failed to thrive even though their physical needs were being met.

When children become fearful of depending upon parents or caretakers who seem cold, distant, self-absorbed, or violent, they naturally retreat to another realm. At the same time, in an effort to protect themselves from the pain of feeling unloved, they may develop protective habits and chronic muscular contractions that end up blocking awareness of the love inside.

Eventually these defensive maneuvers become so familiar it's hard to imagine life without them. These defenses also function to keep the loving vibration of others from getting in. As adults, we no longer depend upon physical contact with others to meet our survival needs, though it's still very pleasurable and health-enhancing! Nevertheless, this habit of seeking love outside ourselves remains, along with the barriers to allowing ourselves to be loved by others. Sometimes we end up confusing love with sex and so our search for love becomes a never ending search for more and better sex.

The quest for love is doomed from the outset for those of us who were actively taught from an early age that love comes from outside. It doesn't matter whether we believe that the source of love is God in heaven, a romantic partner, Mom and Dad, or chocolate ice cream. If we think love is separate from who we are, we're in trouble of one kind or another. You are probably better off believing that love comes from God than from Mom, Dad, or a romantic partner, unless your God tells you you're a sinner who doesn't deserve love. Chocolate ice cream will never judge you or reject you, but it is fattening! In the end, you'll be much better off if you simply acknowledge that *you* are love!

The great mystery is the enormous resistance we have to shifting our attention from the outer world of people and objects to the source of love inside. As we shall see in the next chapter, love flows toward you naturally once you access the love that you are!

Body Armor

When life experiences cause you to lose touch with the love inside, you're likely to develop protective habits and chronic muscular contractions that prevent you from feeling the love inside, and that block the energy of love from penetrating your fearful being. They can also result in a wide variety of physical problems. Your chest caves in or puffs out, your shoulders hunch forward, your belly grows tight, your lips become stiff or turn downward, your chin juts out, your forehead wrinkles or your jaw clenches. Over time, these uncomfortable and unhealthy postures become second nature. They are called *body armor.* If you completely forget you assumed the body armor to avoid the pain of feeling unloved, you're in big trouble—because you've also forgotten that you can choose to release it.

Worse yet, you may take on responsibility for the absence of parental love. "I must be bad or wrong or they would love me. There is something defective in me. I am not enough." Or maybe, "I am too much." Again, these thoughts become unconscious background noise. You forget you are thinking them, but each time you do, they become a bigger barrier to love.

Meanwhile, these undermining thoughts and feelings become entwined with the body armor you've unconsciously created to avoid them. The body armor and the thoughts and feelings reinforce each other, keeping the pattern of feeling unloved firmly in place.

EXERCISE:

Pay close attention to what happens in your body when you tell yourself that you are unlovable or that you will never be loved. Notice your breathing and how you hold your body. Notice any movements you make. Notice your facial expression. Exaggerate all of this. Now see if you can relax completely and deepen your breath. If any emotions come to the surface, allow them to be expressed. Now tell yourself that love is abundant. Imagine yourself floating in a vast warm ocean of love. With each breath, focus on breathing in more love, more energy, more vitality. Put one hand on the center of your chest and one on the center of your belly. Again, pay close attention to what happens in your body. Notice how your posture changes or how you move your body.

The Pitfalls of Falling In Love

The strongest conditioning most of us get is to expect a romantic partner to be the ultimate source of love. Women in particular are led to believe that finding the right man delivers the keys to the kingdom of love. Hundreds of love songs of the "I need your love, can't live without you baby" variety constantly fill the airwaves. Put this together with the nature of sexual interactions that briefly bring to the surface your core self, leading you to mistake your own core of love for a gift that comes from the embodied lover beside you, and it's no wonder that so many of us are confused.

I remember the first time I experienced the euphoric state commonly known as "falling in love." I was twenty-three years old, and thought I'd been in love several times already, but one doesn't know what one doesn't know. I thought that the songs and poetry about this mysterious state of romantic love were fantasy or myth—something made up. It was only after several romances and one marriage that my previous tastes of this condition were revealed to be relatively superficial.

This overwhelming feeling crept up on me over a period of several days leaving me happy but dazed. The earth itself seemed alive and literally moved beneath my feet each time my beloved touched me. When I looked into his eyes, I heard bells ring, and my heart expanded so wide it felt as if it were cracking open. Everything I laid eyes on shimmered with a beauty so intense I could hardly bear it. I lost my appetite. Food seemed unnecessary when each breath I took nourished my soul. I felt a sense of peace, calm, and joy I had never known. Fear, a familiar companion, disappeared.

What I'd called love before seemed bland and uninspiring in comparison. In retrospect I realized that my beloved ignited this experience of transcendent love in me at least in part because his own heart had been blown wide open. He later described to me a spiritual awakening several years before we met which had radically changed his self awareness. I now know that mystics throughout the ages have described their encounters with the Divine in language which echoes that of romantic and erotic love. At the time I only knew that something huge had happened to me—and I thought it was all about him.

From the first time he touched me, gently stroking my bare arm in an attentive but undemanding way, I realized I'd stumbled on undiscovered territory. Up until then, I'd only been touched by people who wanted something. There were men who wanted to seduce me, or impress me, or marry me. Some were lost in pornographic fantasy, others worried about whether they knew what they were doing, or if they were performing well.

Women, starting with Mommy, had yearnings too. They communicated their needs to be loved and appreciated as well as their insecurities and craving for reassurance through touch. I'm sure I was not alone in having rarely, if ever, experienced touch that was not agenda-driven!

This new love transformed my sexuality. Sex had always been a spiritual experience for me, but I'd never known it could be like this. We flowed together effortlessly on many dimensions, becoming one being, and that was only the beginning. For without saying a word about it, he somehow communicated to me that he was worshipping the Divine and that I was She. At that time, nearly thirty years ago, the idea that I was a goddess was a completely new concept for me. Fortunately, this knowledge came in through my body, not my mind, and felt very, very good. It totally bypassed the resistance I would certainly have felt to acknowledging—mentally—what I now know to be true.

Instead, and quite predictably, my mind decided that I had found my soul mate, and immediately began planning a future of blissful togetherness. But it was not to be. I was already committed to attending graduate school a thousand miles away. Even if I'd been willing to change my plans, which I was not, he wasn't exactly begging me not to go. Our bodies and souls fit together—beautifully but our personalities did not.

Our deep friendship has lasted to this day, but when we physically parted ways several months after first meeting, I felt completely bereft. At the same time, my beloved's absence propelled me into a lifelong search for the source of the love I'd first discovered through our encounter. For this I am eternally grateful. Had we stayed together it would have undoubtedly taken many more years for me to find the impetus to look within.

Longing for Love

It's totally human to long for love. Often this longing first appears as a tremendous desire to connect with a particular romantic partner. If this longing is fulfilled, you may be content for a time and look no further. If you are frustrated in your efforts to attract, or keep, the affection of the man or woman of your dreams, you may be more motivated to investigate the source of this longing. Either way, you will eventually come face to face with this mystery. What is this longing for love? Why is it so powerful? Where does it come from? And how can it be satisfied?

Spiritual teachers from every tradition have always told us that you can only long for that which you already are. It appears that the love is in someone else, but this is only an illusion. Sooner or later, you will discover this for yourself. The love that you feel is inside, it can't be felt any other way. If you didn't already know love intimately, you would not long for it. You wouldn't even suspect its existence. If you have never tasted chocolate, you do not crave it. Once you have sampled its delights, you want more. And once you've had fine chocolate, nothing less will satisfy you.

Somehow, most of us have forgotten that we are pure love and so we seek it outside ourselves. This longing is very useful in that it serves to activate your quest for love. Ultimately this search for the beloved leads you to the realization that you feel love when you *are being* loving, not when you are being loved by another.

EXERCISE:

This simple but powerful exercise was suggested by one of my favorite teachers who goes by the name of Adyashanti.[3] Try it yourself and see what happens. The next time you feel that yearning for love, feel backwards into it. Feel it going in, even as it's going out. Feel back, trace it back to its root and see if you don't already possess what you seek. Take it as a question. Is it true that love is absent? Maybe love is abundantly here inside you, or maybe it's just a little bit. Each time the longing for love arises, do this practice with great diligence.

Loving Yourself

One day, a client called me in tears. As she put it, her latest prince had turned out to be a frog. Linda despairingly expressed the fear that there are no good men out there. Instead of reassuring her that the world is full of fabulous men eager to be loved by her, I suggested that she would do well to immerse herself in the love inside herself rather than pursuing romance. "I do great at loving myself," Linda replied, "but I want a man to hold me."

"I'm not talking about loving yourself," I responded, "I'm talking about finding the source of love inside of you."

"What do you mean?" she asked, clearly puzzled. Like many women, Linda had been paying lip service to this new idea while continuing to believe that love comes from a romantic partner.

"When you find the love within you, it will also manifest in loving relationships," I told her. "You can't fake it, and until you become your own source of love your neediness will repel instead of attract love into your life."

Treating yourself with kindness and compassion is certainly a positive step. Eating well, exercising, appreciating yourself, indulging in special treats, and self-care rituals will definitely improve your well-being. But doing these things is not the same as finding the source of love inside. Acting from a mental conviction that nurturing oneself is good for you is not equivalent to a heart-felt outpouring of self-love.

EXERCISE:

The First Time Ever I Saw Your Face. I've used this exercise for many years to help people get access to the love inside. Find a warm, quiet and comfortable place where you won't be disturbed while you close your eyes, relax your body, and listen to this classic love song recorded by Roberta Flack. As you listen to the recording, bring to mind someone you have loved very deeply. Allow yourself to feel all the passion and adoration and devotion you have for this person. Feel the gratitude and vulnerability and excitement of being together. Totally enjoy this feeling of being in love. Now turn this big love around and shine it on yourself. Give *yourself* the same intensity of love you feel for the "love of your life." If you find this difficult or impossible to do, notice what's in the way.

Scarcity vs. Abundance

When you believe that there is not enough love to go around and that you will not get the love you need, your body reacts with fear or anxiety as it would if you were in danger. You shrink into yourself in an effort to get away from this alien, unfriendly and threatening world. If a little love should happen to flow your way, you attempt to cling to it and defend your claim to it with ferocious zeal. Like a miser hoarding his stash of valuables, you are careful to keep others away from the treasure you depend upon for survival.

When you cultivate a sense of abundant love, drinking in the comfort and security of knowing you are held to the bosom of the Divine Mother, your body feels more expansive and open. You know there is plenty of love for everyone, so you can freely give it away. You have a sense of being at home and provided for wherever you find yourself, so you become more outgoing and friendly. You want to share your sense of abundance with others who also feel this abundance. You have a choice. Which feels better to you? Which reality do you prefer?

A Course in Miracles defines sin as "lack of love."[4] When we look at the behaviors and attitudes which stem from a belief in the scarcity of love, this definition makes a lot of sense. Depression, anxiety, jealousy, envy, addiction, greed, and selfishness can all be seen to have their roots in the experience of not having enough love. Instead of viewing the sin of perceiving scarcity as an evil to be punished, the Course sees sin as a mistaken perception, which can be changed by seeing more clearly that you have an endless supply of love in your very own heart.

Addiction and the Need for Approval

The mistaken belief that love comes from someone or someplace outside, and the perception that inside there is only emptiness, often leads to addiction. In order to avoid the disappointment of feeling unloved and the agonizing emptiness inside, many people turn to substances or activities which make them feel good temporarily, or at least dull their awareness of what they imagine they are lacking. Occasional use may be a pleasant distraction from suffering, but whether one turns to alcohol, drugs, work, drama, control, sex, or relationships, if you depend on your chosen addiction to mask the feeling of being unloved, you deprive yourself of the motivation to find the source of love inside.

Relying on a substance or activity to avoid the feeling of being unloved keeps you stuck. It's virtually impossible to extricate yourself from a trap you don't know that you're in. It's as if your pockets were filled with rocks. You wonder why each step that you take requires so much effort. You complain about how stuck you feel. Meanwhile these heavy rocks begin to wear holes in your pockets, but instead of letting the rocks fall out, you expend even more energy trying to keep the holes mended.

Perhaps the most common addiction of all is the addiction to approval. This addiction to approval is so prevalent in our society that it seems quite normal, but this is only because we've forgotten the Law of Source. When you believe that love comes from outside, and that in order to receive this love you must meet certain conditions, you are at risk for becoming addicted to approval. This need for approval keeps you in a childlike state of dependency.

Instead of teaching our children to cultivate the ability to validate themselves, we train them to seek validation from others. When it isn't forthcoming, panic ensues. The giving and receiving of validation is even put forth by many marriage counselors as a strategy for healthy relationships.

It's certainly pleasant to receive validation from your partner, just as a glass of wine with dinner can be pleasant. If you are able to skip the wine, or the approval, when it's not available, you can choose to enjoy it when it's offered. Otherwise you have no choice. You must have it. Like all addictions, the need for approval limits your freedom to act with total integrity. If you're addicted to approval, you will sell your soul for it. You're incapable of making a choice which might prove unpopular.

Control

Much of the conflict in love relationships arises from one person attempting to control another. Individual differences are inevitable. People have different desires, different needs, different tastes, different opinions, different beliefs, different values, different priorities, and different points of view.

Differences do not have to mean conflict. If you approach differences as valid and intriguing qualities, to be creatively blended, or separately enjoyed and expressed, harmony can prevail.

What often happens instead is that we see differences as threats that may prevent access, or continued access, to our perceived source of love. We counter this danger by taking action to control the other. We may do it indirectly through manipulation, sulking, or threatening to withdraw our own love and support. We may do it directly by issuing orders, ultimatums, or polite requests which are really demands. Or we may keep ourselves separate and alone in an effort to avoid the whole issue.

A simple request, if it can be declined without adverse reaction, may not carry the intent to control. But a request may also be a demand, cloaked in the costume of choice. One man I knew was so wary of being controlled that he would routinely decline requests just to see what the reaction would be to his refusal to comply. If his "no" was not met with gracious acceptance, he immediately prepared for battle. If the battle was not won instantaneously, he bolted from the relationship.

Many people have an automatic unconscious resistance to demands. If you're intent upon getting love from your partner, he will probably experience this as a demand. Without even being conscious of it, he may resist giving you what you want. Or he may give it grudgingly, resentful that he couldn't give it freely because of your insistence.

When two people engage with the conscious or unconscious intent to control one another, a power struggle ensues. How sad! How futile! We've all done this enough to know that it doesn't work. As we shall see in the next chapter, the reality is that the power struggle very effectively prevents both parties from coming together and staying together in a loving way.

Instead, remember that the urge to control the other is a misguided attempt to get more love, or to control the imagined source of your love. Fortunately, this struggle is completely unnecessary. The love resides in your own heart. It is freely available to you at all times and does not depend upon controlling your partner.

Chapter Three
The Law of Attraction

If you fill your heart with love and gratitude, you will find yourself surrounded by so much that you can love and that you can feel grateful for. But what will happen if you emit signals of hate, dissatisfaction, and sadness? Then you will probably find yourself in a situation that makes you hateful, dissatisfied, and sad. — MASARU EMOTO, The Hidden Messages in Water

The Law of Attraction simply means that like attracts like. This law is the most basic of all natural laws. The Law of Attraction applies to every aspect of our lives, including love and relationships. The Law of Attraction tells us that if we want to draw love into our lives, we must find *and express* the love inside ourselves. If we emanate love we will attract love. This is equally true for any other state of mind. If we are angry, we attract anger. If we are critical, we attract criticism. If we feel abundant, we attract abundance, and if we are empathic we attract empathy.

Every spiritual tradition has some version of this law. In the Christian tradition it's known as the Golden Rule: Do unto others as you would have others do unto you. The Hawaiians, who call it *Kanawee Mo'aka'aka,* say that in ancient Hawaii it was the only law necessary. This is because everyone understood that you get what you give. No other law was needed. With this knowledge, people naturally act in harmony with the good of the whole. Why would you harm someone if you realized that you are only hurting yourself in the end?

My dear friends Armand and Angelina, who have provided music for many of my workshops, have written a song called *Love Is a Boomerang.*[5] The lyrics say, "Give it away and it comes right back." This is another simple expression of the Law of Attraction. Of course, love is not really an object, like a boomerang, that can be given away, or tossed in the air, but this image helps to convey how the energy that you send out bounces right back. This is why blame and defensiveness so effectively work against attracting love into your life.

Because love is a boomerang, if you treat others with kindness and consideration, you will eventually find kindness and consideration coming your way. However, if your motivation to be loved leads you act lovingly *in order to be loved,* you may not get the result you want. Manipulation attracts more manipulation, not love. The more you manipulate, the more you will be resented.

It doesn't matter whether you believe in the Law of Attraction or not. Like gravity it operates all day, every day. Depending upon the time and place, the turnaround may be instantaneous, or there may be a delay, but it will definitely arrive. Don't take my word for it. Try it out for yourself and see what happens.

The War between the Sexes

The Law of Attraction helps to explain why people frequently feel unloved, even when they are in committed relationships. It also explains why love is only possible between those who see each other as equals. What often passes for love in marriages, or other long term romantic relationships, is actually a negotiated truce in the war between the sexes.

Men and women need each other to reproduce and often rely upon the other for sex, romantic excitement, and support of various kinds. There are happy exceptions, but trust, respect, and honest communication between men and women have not been the norm for a long, long time. The story underlying the centuries old war between the sexes is not a love story. Rather, it is a story of fear, cruelty, conflict, and struggle for survival. It is a story of enemies who each attempt to get the upper hand in order to meet their basic and divergent needs. It is a story of how men and women deceive, manipulate and take advantage of each other.

"If you let me call the shots in this relationship, and do whatever I want, I will protect you and your children and provide for you." Or, "I will nurture and support you and give you exclusive rights to sex with me, if you make all the decisions and take responsibility for our worldly survival."

This kind of negotiation determines who will be the dominant party and who will be the submissive party in a couple. In our culture we usually associate feminine with the submissive role and masculine with the dominant role, but either gender can take either role. If each keeps their side of the bargain it can create a stable relationship, at least for a time. But according to the Law of Attraction, a relationship based on power dynamics and economics, rather than love freely shared between equals, will generate ongoing power exchanges, not love.

We are so thoroughly indoctrinated to believe that romance, sexual attraction, dependency, and power dynamics are a satisfactory basis for love that we never question this erroneous assumption! Both domination and submission attract love's opposite, namely resentment and separation.

As author Riane Eisler[6] so brilliantly documents, for over two millennia, relationships between men and women have been based on a hierarchical, authoritarian model in which the threat of painful punishment is used to maintain the status quo. It makes no difference which gender is on top; force begets force and pain begets pain, not love.

Assuming a heterosexual relationship[7] based on power dynamics, both men and women have the same two options: they can be dominant or they can be submissive.[8] Dominance and submission are complementary. They are like two puzzle pieces that fit together perfectly. This is an instance where it appears that opposites attract. But both dominant and submissive partners are playing the same game. They are two sides of the same coin.

If two dominants come together, they will struggle for dominance until one of them submits or goes away. If two submissives come together they will also struggle for the submissive position until one of them accepts the dominant position or one of them goes away. These pairings are rare, but may occur when both parties are in the midst of transcending the game of "who's on top?" and revert to their old habits.

So what we are usually left with is a couple where one person plays the dominant role and the other plays the submissive. This may work for awhile, especially if there is some flexibility about which role is played. But if the expected outcome is love, disappointment is inevitable.

In these power-based relationships, what is offered is a promise to fulfill the other's needs providing certain conditions are met. There's nothing inherently wrong with this kind of arrangement, but it is not, and can not be, experienced as love. We may call it love, but in reality it's a business arrangement. On a gut level, it will be experienced as such.

The Dominant Man & the Submissive Woman

If the man takes the dominant role, as is considered most desirable in our culture, he seeks a woman who will look up to him, who will support him in all his endeavors, and who will subordinate her own needs and desires to his own. As one dominant man put it, "When we are together it's all about me and how I like things to be and that's how I want it."

At first, a submissive woman will be thrilled that she's found a strong, powerful man to protect her. She delights in charming him with her sexual allure, which excites them both temporarily, but creates a superficial connection. Even if she has a career, she presents herself as the perfect helper, an ideal wife and mother.

Underneath, she may be afraid of men. She's learned they can be cruel and dangerous. She avoids speaking her truth if it might create conflict. She pretends to be more sexually responsive than she really feels. Her sexuality is all on the surface and she wonders deep down if she is really adequate as a woman. In the shadow of his life, she loses her sense of herself and feels lost and confused. She begins to resent him for controlling her and dreads his physical or emotional abuse if she asserts her individuality. Eventually she may feel she has to leave him in order to find herself.

Meanwhile, the man is increasingly frustrated by his inability to make deep contact with the woman. She offers herself outwardly, but she can't really receive him. She becomes more and more distant. It's as if he were reaching for a mirage. Worst yet, she can't give him what he most needs, which is the validation for his own masculinity, because he doesn't have much respect for her. She's only a woman. The only meaningful validation for him has to come from another man.

A dominant man most often had a father who was insecure in his masculinity and had to prove his worth by constantly competing with other men, including his son. Like his father before him, the son didn't get the male support he desperately needed because the father viewed him as a threat to be battled for the attention of the boy's mother. The father boosts his own ego by belittling the son, and the pattern is passed down through the generations.

Likewise, the submissive woman often had a mother who didn't support the daughter's feminine expression. Such a woman is insecure in her own power as a woman. This kind of mother may be jealous of her husband's attention to the daughter and try to come in between them. She is threatened by her daughter's innocent sexuality and may punish it, because she feels cut off from her own. A woman like this must try very hard to appear feminine and sexy to make up for her inner doubts. She desperately needs the support of other women, but has trouble getting it because her experience is one of competition with women to win the prize of attention from the male. This pattern is also passed down through the generations.

The Dominant Woman & the Submissive Man

The dominance-submission dance doesn't work any better the other way around. If a woman takes the dominant role, she will come across as a strong, decisive, take-charge kind of person. She is often very successful in her career and knows how to get things done. A submissive man is drawn to her power and admires her abilities. "What a Goddess you are," he gushes, "how can I serve you?" He uses his charm and nurturing qualities to court her. She is thrilled at first, thinking that at last she's found a man who is supportive of her and who appreciates and values her independence. All is well for awhile, but sooner or later she gets angry. Suddenly her power frightens him. He reacts by withdrawing. Like his mother, she is too demanding, too controlling, and too critical. Or perhaps his mother was overprotective and smothering. Either way, the submissive man didn't get the feminine support he needed in childhood.

Overwhelmed by his partner, he begins to back away. He desperately wants and needs the love of the feminine, but his distrust of the feminine has him see-sawing between humiliating dependency and sullen withholding. Often, he is repeating the pattern of a wishy-washy and insecure father who had similar problems with women.

The man's withdrawal triggers the woman's rage toward the father who didn't give her what she wanted or needed. Whether he neglected or abandoned her, or was abusive and angry himself, in some way he wasn't there for her, and consequently she finds it hard to trust men. She expects men to let her down, to disappoint her, to sabotage her. Her anger and resentment grows with each experience of failure. As she gets angrier her partner becomes more and more distant. Each feeds the other's worst fears in a cycle of despair.

The Only Way Out Is In

In each of these scenarios, the internal dynamic of both partners is one of separation, fear, and mistrust. This attracts a partner who mirrors the same dynamics. The Law of Attraction tells us that this is inevitable, but it also points the way to love. Yes, we can attract more love into our lives, even with this kind of history. But it requires that we create a more respectful and supportive relationship between the feminine and masculine *within*. Then, the harmony we feel inside will attract a more harmonious partner.

How can you create this inner harmony? Many paths will lead you there and a complete discussion of them all is beyond the scope of this book. In fact, one might say that this harmonizing of *internal polarities* is the essence of most spiritual practices. What many paths have in common is the recognition that generating harmony involves internal transformation. If you have no idea how to begin, keep your awareness on these questions and affirm your willingness to receive answers. Be prepared to attract a teacher who is perfect for you, and do your best to recognize her when she appears.

Remember, even if it were possible to change your partner, according to the Law of Attraction, this would merely serve to attract a more loving counterpart *for your partner*. Fixing your partner, as desirable as that might seem, will never heal your inner conflicts and it will not bring more love into your life. The Law of Attraction suggests that the key is putting your attention on yourself and your own internal experience. When you earnestly and lovingly look inside instead of pointing the finger of blame at your partner (or yourself), you're much more likely to attract the love you want. Remember, blame only serves to attract more blame!

Forget about your partner and whatever he or she has or hasn't done. If you are suffering, be with that pain. Be willing to feel your hurt and anger completely without making any effort to change it. This is the only way to release these emotions so that they stop attracting more of the same!

See if you can notice older, earlier layers of emotions which have been triggered by your current experience. To the best of your ability, totally accept your present situation and cultivate compassion (not pity) for yourself. This is not about martyrdom or masochism! If you are still on the receiving end of abusive behavior, state clearly that this is unacceptable to you and remove yourself from the situation if necessary. Notice any tendency you may have to enjoy your suffering. Just be curious and as aware as you can be without evaluating or analyzing your reactions.

EXERCISE:

Rewriting Your Family History. This exercise is derived from Dr. Jack Painter's Pelvic Heart Integration work and utilizes psychodrama techniques to help harmonize the relationship between your Inner Man and Inner Woman. It's best done in a small group so that other people can play the roles you assign them while you experience the effect, but you could also do it as a guided fantasy or journaling exercise.

If you are working in a group, begin by choosing someone to play your mother and someone to play your father. If you have a family of origin which includes multiple fathers or mothers, for example, you are adopted, or you have a step-parent, you can include all of them. If you are working alone, simply bring your parents to mind or draw a circle or figure to represent each one.

Now, remember back to when you were a small child. What kind of messages (both spoken and unspoken) did you get from each parent about relationships with the opposite sex? What body postures went with these messages? Either write these down, cartoon-style, or share them with your psychodramatic stand-ins and have them repeat the message to you. Keep it to as few words as possible and be sure to get the tone of voice and facial expressions right.

Next, ask yourself, "What did your parents feel about each other?" How would you arrange their bodies in space to express this? For example, if they were very distant with each other, you might put them on opposite sides of the room. Arrange the actors or draw them in your journal. Pay attention to what you feel in your body in response to these scenes and messages. Speak or write whatever comes up for you.

Chances are that your early exposure to man-woman relationships was less than ideal. Nevertheless, your parents become your role models and internal templates for your inner masculine and inner feminine. Now you have the opportunity to consciously re-write the script!

Ask yourself, "What messages about love and relationship would you like to have received from an ideal parent, or the divine masculine and feminine?" Never mind if your real parents would never say these things. That doesn't matter. This is for you. Think especially about what you need to hear to help you through any relationship issues which constantly trip you up. Share these with your group or write them down. Again, keep it simple. Listen to these words spoken aloud. Breathe. Let them sink in. Remember that you can repeat these messages to yourself any time you want.

How would you like to see your ideal parents interacting with each other? What position would their bodies take. What would they say to each other? Where would you be in this picture? Now arrange the actors or draw this configuration. See how this feels in your body. Make any adjustments that would make it even better. Breathe.

Gratitude

To complete the healing process, it's important to follow the re-experiencing of past hurt and anger with the cultivation of gratitude. In this way you can balance whatever complaints turned up by discovering the gifts concealed in your relationship challenges.

The Law of Attraction tells us that the more you focus on love and gratitude, the more love and gratitude you will attract. Just remember that until you acknowledge and release conflicting emotions, such as anger or hatred, they may override your conscious intent. Once you've made space for your thornier feelings, make an effort to find things to be grateful for. Find ways you have appreciated significant people in your life. This may feel forced or phony at first, but sometimes "faking it until you make it" works.

The power of gratitude can literally be seen in the innovative research of Masaru Emoto. Incredible as it sounds, he has ascertained that when water is shown the written words love and gratitude it forms beautiful crystals which are undamaged by magnetic fields which alter the crystals formed by untreated water. While the word love alone creates wonderful crystals, when love is combined with gratitude the crystals have "a unique depth and refinement" and "diamond-like brilliance."[9]

He interprets his findings as evidence that gratitude has an even stronger influence than love. Dr. Emoto goes on to say that "Love tends to be a more active energy, the act of giving oneself unconditionally. By contrast, gratitude is a more passive energy, a feeling that results from having been given something—knowing that you have been given the gift of life and reaching out to receive it joyously with both hands."[10]

If we understand gratitude to be the receptive form of love, the immense power of gratitude to attract love can be easily understood. While our culture has emphasized the active mode over the receptive mode for thousands of years, ancient cultures knew that the capacity to magnetize the desired result yields amazing benefits—with far less expenditure of effort than active pursuit.

The paradox of gratitude is this. In order to attract what you want, you need to feel grateful for what you already have. If you focus on what you lack, and how much you want what you don't have, you will attract more wanting and more lacking. If instead you can see yourself as so filled with love that you are overflowing, and feel grateful for this gift, you'll no longer be concerned about what you're going to get. You've already got it.

Resonance

Another way to think about the Law of Attraction is to think of each emotional state, each life form, and each individual as having a certain frequency. This idea is found in spiritual teachings from many traditions. In other words, we are all vibrating at different frequencies, and some of these frequencies resonate, or amplify each other, and others do not. This is what is meant by the expression, "You're on my wavelength." As in music, some frequencies harmonize and some create dissonance. Change your frequency by consistently changing your emotional state, and you will attract a different type of person.

As any hypnotist can tell you, the subconscious world of vibration does not understand the word *not*. This is why the Law of Attraction operates to draw in whatever it is that you fear or resist. If you focus on what you don't want, or don't like, you are amplifying that vibration, and that's what you will attract. This is why the woman who is afraid that the man won't be there for her, or the man who is afraid the woman will be controlling and smothering, will resonate with those partners who will perfectly fulfill their fears.

If we allow ourselves to be guided by the vibrational cues of the Law of Attraction, as opposed to visual cues or mental constructs, we are naturally drawn to those people whose frequencies match our own. This can be disconcerting at times, especially if you don't like the reflection of yourself that you see in the other, but this is how we grow!

Chapter Four
The Law of Unity

Love takes no position, and thus is global, rising above separation. It's then possible to be 'with one another,' for there are no longer any barriers. Love is therefore inclusive and expands the sense of self progressively. Love focuses on the goodness of life in all its expressions and augments that which is positive—it dissolves negativity by recontextualizing it, rather than by attacking it.
—DAVID HAWKINS, Power vs. Force

The fourth law of love is the Law of Unity. The Law of Unity tells us that love embraces all. Love includes everything and everyone. In love there is no separation, there is no "us" and no "them." There is only One. Love is not against some things and for others. Love has no agenda, love simply is.

Like the sweet scent of a flower floating on the breeze, love is available to whoever receives it. There is no limit to how many souls love can grace. The rose bush does not ask, "Who is this passing by my garden? Will I permit them a whiff of my fragrance?" Neither does the rose bush worry, "Is every passerby getting my perfume? Did the wind carry it away too fast?"

The Law of Unity is relatively easy to describe but perhaps the most challenging of all the laws of love to apply to every day life. How is it possible to have a partner and a family and still love everybody? What does it really mean to embrace everything? Is there no place at all in love for boundaries and distinctions?

The dualistic nature of the mind, which automatically slices life into categories of good/bad, right/wrong, and love/hate, finds the very idea of oneness alien and threatening. It immediately begins building a case against unity, telling us this kind of love is impractical, burdensome, utopian, and even sinful.

Just as I was beginning to write this chapter the phone rang. My intention was to focus exclusively on writing for the next hour, but when I saw that the caller was a friend and colleague I'd been trying to reach for days, I found myself reaching for the phone.

"I'm working on my book right now" I told him. "Can I call you back in an hour?" He said that I could call but would probably be unable to reach him, so I chose to delay my writing and speak with him right away.

After I hung up the phone, I noticed that my mind was struggling to reconcile the gap between my intention and my action. Was taking the phone call the most loving thing to do for myself and my friend? Was I practicing the Law of Unity? Was I embracing whatever showed up, just as I was writing about it? Was I trusting that sharing my time would not mean that there wasn't enough time left to meet my writing goal for the day?

Or was I foolishly allowing myself to be separated from what I really wanted and needed to be doing? Was I failing to stick with my intention? Would I ever finish this book if I allowed myself to be interrupted? Was I giving up my own agenda to suit someone else?

The answer to these questions is contained in the tone with which they were delivered. The words "foolishly" and "failing" suggest a critical and judgmental attitude. Fear and doubt contrast sharply with the trust and openness which accompanied my original impulse to be more flexible with my time. Despite the concerns my mind brought forward, I felt satisfied and at peace with my decision to answer the phone.

Does this mean that it's always more loving to put your own timing aside to suit someone else? Absolutely not! A couple of days later I was again sitting down to write when the phone rang. I picked it up and noticed I felt irritated and distracted, and quickly told the caller I'd be available later, but not now.

This time, I knew immediately that taking the call was not in alignment with love. Had I stayed on the phone and ignored my gut feeling that the call was interfering with path, my resentment would have grown unmanageable and I probably would have ended up snapping at my friend. Instead, my friend appreciated and understood my need to be left alone (although it wouldn't have changed anything if he didn't) and I was able to go with my creative flow.

Similarly, there are times when multi-tasking (doing several things at once) feels exhilarating, expansive, and efficient. At other times, it feels stressful and distracting. The point is to notice what feels right to you at a particular time, rather than rigidly and automatically adhering to a rule which says include everything and everybody all the time.

Inclusion

The struggle with inclusion often arises at the onset of an activity requiring a lot of centering, like meditation or lovemaking. Has this ever happened to you? You begin to focus attention on quieting the mind. You deepen your breath and relax your body. You become aware of your internal sensations. A pleasant state of concentration or arousal is just starting to develop when a baby's cry, the shrill ring of a telephone, a passing motorcycle, or some other noise, pierces the silence.

What to do? If you're a parent and your baby needs you, you will of course respond to the call for attention. If this is not the case, you have a choice. You can get annoyed by the distracting noises and go into complaint mode. "It should be quiet. I don't want to be interrupted by these sounds. Damn these inconsiderate people!"

On and on it goes until your resistance to the distraction has completely derailed your intended experience. Or you can include whatever sounds are present into your meditation or lovemaking. The ring of the telephone can become an opportunity to breathe deeper and relax more completely. The baby's cry could be a joyful reminder of your love. You could try imagining the vibration of the motorcycle traveling up your spine.

EXERCISE:

A great way to increase your skills at inclusion is to practice meditating or focusing on love while a yellowjacket or wasp is buzzing around you. This may sound odd but it works! Use whatever meditative style you prefer, or just pay attention to slow, regular breathing, and radiating love from the center of your chest. See if you can peacefully include the presence of the yellowjacket or even silently invite it to stay with you. If you do this well, the yellowjacket will probably leave in a hurry, as they seem to be more attracted to angry or fearful energy than to love.

Monogamy and the Law of Unity

Another area where confusion about inclusion often arises has to do with sexual attractions outside the couple. How can the Law of Unity and an understanding of the inclusive nature of love be reconciled with the practice of monogamy?

First of all, it's important to realize that love is not sex and sex is not love. A commitment to be sexually monogamous does not preclude feeling and expressing love for people other than your partner.

As we discussed in Chapter One, it is useless to try to dictate when, where, and with whom love will appear. Sometimes the feeling of love ignites sexual attraction between people, but love will not push blindly ahead to express itself sexually without consideration for all those who might be affected. At the same time, love does not try to prevent sexual feelings from arising, nor does love hide the truth of its passion. Neither does love bow down to the demands of anyone's ego.

Some people may choose not to include sexual contact with more than one person into their bonds of love, while freely acknowledging any other attractions that arise. Others may decide to try intimate relating that goes beyond the couple. Either way, as long as you are honestly sharing the truth about feelings and actions with all those involved, you're in alignment with the Law of Unity.

If instead you try to prevent, avoid, or hide your attraction or love for others, you're courting disaster. This effort to exclude something—the truth, sexual energy, or love's expansion—will end up strangling love in one way or another. If you are hiding your true feelings, your partner will sense this and react, perhaps without consciously being aware of it. And if you try to force your energy to flow only toward your partner, it will slowly dry up and die, like a wild river channeled into a shallow concrete ditch.

Spiritual teacher Byron Katie[11] was once asked why she chose to be monogamous even though she didn't believe it to be a moral imperative. Her first response was to say that she wanted to include everyone in her love and that she would have to be insane to think that she could do so by having sex with everyone on the planet. Then after running through a whole list of reasons she ended up saying the reasons were irrelevant. The bottom line was that she just did. This is the way it naturally was for her, but she was wise enough to know it might not be that way for everyone.

It's quite obvious that constraints of time and energy dictate that physical union is necessarily limited to a small number of people, while the joining of hearts and souls is truly unlimited. However, it's important to remember that we are all different in our capacities for experiencing and expressing love.

Someone who is working toward dissolving the barriers which seem to keep them separate even from those they are closest to may make more progress if their sexual union is with only one partner. Those whose sense of unity with all creation is constant and strong may choose to limit their sexual expression to make themselves more available to the world at large. If your journey finds you somewhere in between these extremes, as most of us are, it's important to realize that the Law of Unity can manifest in an infinite variety of ways. This is called unity in diversity.

Polarization

We often think of unity as referring to union with others, but the unity, or lack of unity, *within* is far more important than what happens outside. This is because we usually externalize our inner conflicts. Then we end up struggling with others when the source of the discord is inside. It's difficult to find unity amidst the diversity of the outer world if you haven't found a way to embrace the multiplicity inside your own skin.

For example, let's say that you are conflicted about whether you want to get married or not. You've been told all your life that marriage is the ultimate expression of love and have been planning your wedding since you were a child. The part of you that wants to get married is a part you are comfortable with and feel good about.

Another part of you has doubts about this whole marriage thing. This part has witnessed many painful divorces and angry confrontations between spouses. This part is worried about taking on outdated, traditional sex roles or financial entanglements. This part has heard statistics that the majority of men and women have secret extramarital affairs. You are not so comfortable with the part of yourself who is suspicious and distrustful of marriage. You don't want to listen to what the anti-marriage self has to say because it might get in the way of achieving your goal of marriage.

It's very common for a person with this kind of internal conflict to attract a partner who is their mirror image. In this case, it would be a partner who is consciously against marriage yet also has a deep, unconscious desire to be married. These two fall in love, in part because the other is expressing their secret or hidden self.

Now the conflict becomes an issue in the relationship between them. Every attempt to change the other creates a deeper rift in the relationship. The more stubbornly one insists upon marriage, the more entrenched the other becomes in opposing it. The longer this goes on, the more strongly each identifies with their position and the less likely they are to recognize the validity of the other's point of view. The inner struggle has created a battle with another person. The internal conflict has been projected out into the world.

This relationship is doomed unless at least one of the partners owns both sides of this polarity and begins to work on ending the war going on inside. For example, if the pro-marriage partner takes the conflict back inside and admits that they are also afraid of marriage, the anti-marriage partner has space to acknowledge their desire for marriage without propelling them both to the altar immediately.

If both the pro-marriage and anti-marriage stances can be listened to with respect, and accepted as part of the whole picture, understanding and loving resolution becomes possible. If one partner is able to stop blaming the other and acknowledge the validity of both positions, the opening for a solution exists. Both parties will still have to find a way to inner unity, but now they have an opportunity to lovingly support each other in this endeavor instead of making the other wrong.

Special Relationships

Our religions teach us that God is Love, and that love flows naturally from the heart, but our lives today are anything but natural. In our present-day society, we place a great deal of emphasis on special personal relationships, whether they are romantic, parent-child, or other blood family to a lesser extent simple friendships. These close relationships are the places we designate as appropriate arenas for the expression of love.

This is partly because our lives have grown so complex. In the big cities and suburbs where most of us live and work, we are surrounded by so many people we don't know well that we are overwhelmed. Exposure to still more people through the constant barrage of the mass media exponentially increases the number of people we are confronted with on a daily basis.

Together with the fear and mistrust of strangers that pervades our culture, this creates a climate in which few people approach everyone they encounter with love. We begin to treat the grocery clerk, the mail carrier, the ticket taker at the movie theatre, as nonentities, barely recognizing each other as fellow humans, let alone as beloveds.

In contrast, the "significant other" becomes ever more significant in this ocean of impersonality. Our close personal contacts are the training ground for learning and practicing the art of love. Ultimately, we extend our love, or its opposite, to the world at large. At root, the primary love "object" is oneself. Until we develop the capacity to freely be the love that we are, we aren't capable of truly loving another. The reflection provided by friends, lovers, and family members is a potent means of becoming aware of our beliefs about love.

Most of us have been taught that we are made special through the exclusive attentions bestowed by a significant other. This desire to be loved over and above, beyond anyone or anything else, often begins in childhood, with competition for first place in mother's affection. A parent or a sibling, a hobby or a career, may threaten to eclipse your claim to mother's primary consideration, triggering fears about your very survival.

Later in life, if love continues to be misconstrued as the conferring of exclusive attention, we have a tendency to become jealous and possessive when love flows in other directions. Cultural norms which support these reactions only serve to create more confusion. We are simultaneously shamed for the pettiness of feeling jealous, and assured that jealousy is appropriate and necessary to demonstrate love.

Sometimes, the guarantee of specialness is signified by certain behaviors which are reserved for just the two of you. Sexual intercourse is frequently viewed in this way, but almost anything can become the conveyer of specialness. The emotional reaction activated by a perceived challenge to the special relationship stems from the fear of not being loved, and therefore being alone, separate, and uncared for.

This is why the *A Course in Miracles* teaches that "special relationships" are "destructive, selfish, and childishly egocentric."[12] The solution is not to pretend that everyone is the same and all relationships are equally significant. Nor is it to invoke The Law of Unity as an excuse for avoiding commitment, breaking agreements, or scattering your energy so widely that it loses coherence.

Rather the idea is to use these relationships as a means of becoming more loving, instead of letting special relationships be used to create more separation. In order to do this, we must honor each other as teachers uniquely suited for the expansion of our own capacity for love.

At the same time, we need to remember that the Law of Unity tells us that love is essentially impersonal. Love knows that we are all One. Love knows that we are all special, but love is under no obligation to prove to you that you are special—and will do its best to relieve you of the delusion that you are more special than anyone else. This impersonal quality of love may well be the most challenging for your ego to accept, but until you go beyond the personal, soul-satisfying love will elude you.

Altruism

True love always wants the happiness of the beloved. The choice to unselfishly do something that benefits someone else—even to one's own apparent detriment—is called altruism. Altruism is sometimes viewed as impossibly idealistic and utopian. If you understand the Law of Unity, you see that altruism is consistent with the natural laws of love.

Once you recognize that we are all connected, you understand the joy that comes from helping someone else. It is no different than doing something for yourself except that you also have the enjoyment of serving another and witnessing their happiness. Love's truest expression is in being of service. Altruism is one name we give to love that has no boundaries and no borders.

In the movie *Besieged*[13] a young African woman relocates to Rome to further her education after her husband is thrown into prison for opposing the ruling military regime. She finds work as a live-in housekeeper for a pianist and composer. One day he breaks down and confesses he's in love with her. Overcome with emotion, he tells her he's never felt this way before. He tries to embrace her and begs her to love him in return saying, "I'll do anything to get you to love me, just tell me what I have to do!"

She is frightened and offended by his passion. She pushes him away, screaming, "Get my husband out of jail!"

He turns away, looking stricken, and after a moment replies, "I didn't realize you were married." Nothing more is said on the subject, but as the movie unfolds, the antique sculptures, furniture, paintings, and tapestries begin to disappear from the villa. Then she gets a letter from her husband saying he will soon be released from prison and arriving in Rome. Minutes later she sees the Steinway grand piano being lowered from the window of the composer's house and she realizes he has sold everything, even the piano which is his whole life and livelihood, to get her husband out of prison.

The film ends on an ambiguous note, with the woman telling the pianist that she loves him as her husband arrives at the door. We don't know the outcome, just as the pianist doesn't know what the outcome will be when he lets go of his most precious possession.

We do know that what we have witnessed was not the superficial infatuation or sexual attraction we might have assumed at first. Love has guided him to selflessly fulfill the heartfelt desire of his beloved, even though by doing so it appears he is losing any chance for a love affair with her.

Can you imagine yourself relinquishing everything for the happiness of your beloved? If not, what would prevent you from doing so? That such generosity of spirit and absence of self-centeredness rarely accompanies romantic love shows us how far removed the typical romance is from the law of unity. Altruism is more commonly seen in parental love, but even here unselfishness is often lacking. All the world's great religions emphasize the importance of applying the law of unity to love. For example, Jesus taught "Love your neighbor as yourself." When enough people put this into practice, love will finally prevail!

Chapter Five
The Law of Truth

I was in Chandigarh, India, giving a lecture at the campus of the university there. I walked by a temple, and written just above the front entrance were the words, God Is Truth. *I had certainly heard* God Is Love *before. I was surprised to realize that perhaps truth and love were the same thing.*—FRED ALAN WOLF, The Eagle's Quest

The fifth law of love is the Law of Truth. The Law of Truth tells us that love flourishes in the presence of truth. We use the phrase "true love" as if there could be any other kind of love. This cannot be. There are many things we call love, but they are counterfeits if they are not solidly grounded in truth. The Law of Truth means that love implies a commitment to the truth. This is why Sufi master Hazrat Inayat Khan has said, "If there is truth in anything, it is in love; if there is not truth in love there is not truth in anything."[14]

Love cannot be based on lies. Deception, pretense, and illusion are potent ways to keep love away. Have you ever noticed that whenever someone honestly expresses whatever they are feeling—with no blame, defensiveness, self-deception or hidden agenda—you feel a surge of love? Even if what's been said is not what you wanted to hear, the very act of vulnerable self-disclosure draws love like a magnet.

The truth opens hearts where ever it lands. The more truth is shared, the more love expands, but even a little bit of truth can make a difference. Letting others know what's happening in your inner world helps them to understand you and empathize with you. This is why it's often said that truth is the greatest aphrodisiac.

Nevertheless, many people find it difficult to believe that telling the truth creates more love. If you're convinced that you're unlovable just the way you are, you dare not risk letting anyone see the real you. Like a woman who believes she's not beautiful without her make-up, you feel you must hide behind layer after layer of cosmetic cover-ups. Those who sell cosmetics are only too happy to reinforce this belief.

If you believe that your beauty comes from artificial sources, you won't take my word, or anyone else's, that you are naturally attractive. But maybe one day, you're in such a rush you barely have time to brush your hair. To make matters worse, you've been crying and your eyelids are slightly puffy. You feel vulnerable and exposed going out with your face bare. Much to your surprise, everyone you meet tells you that you look especially beautiful today. You scrutinize each person suspiciously to see if they're being sarcastic, but no, they appear to be sincere. The unthinkable has happened and it's thrown your whole picture of yourself into question.

Perhaps something similar has happened to you on an emotional level. The stress, or grief, or anger you are carrying becomes so great it overwhelms you. The mask cracks and you can't help showing your real feelings, even with people you don't know very well. You are shocked to discover that instead of rejection, your distress is met with sympathy and kindness. You feel supported and cared for. Your belief that you cannot be loved if you reveal your true self begins to crumble. You begin to wonder whether the ones who've taught you to hide your true feelings and thoughts have been misguided. Is it really in your best interest to deny the truth of your being?

The conditioning which most of us have gotten is the exact opposite of the Law of Truth. The man-made version could be stated like this: If you want to be loved you must project an image of perfection and never say anything which might hurt someone's feelings. Never show weakness, and never be impolite. Never reveal family secrets. Lie if you need to in order to make a good impression, and keep quiet about anything controversial.

If you've been trained to lie about your real feelings and needs from an early age, being truly intimate may be a challenge for you, even if you've personally experienced the powerful relationship between truth-telling and love. The aversion to truth-telling is partly habit, but it persists for two reasons. First, in order to speak the truth, you have to know the truth. Second, you have to give up trying to control the outcome of speaking the truth.

The best way to lie to others is to lie to oneself. After many years of lying to yourself, you may no longer know your true feelings and thoughts. Possibly, you don't even know when you're lying to yourself. You want to be authentic but you've forgotten how. Your internal censor has hidden the key to your house of secrets and you don't know where to find it. Here's a clue: Pay attention to what's happening right now. Learn to access reality in present time before your censor gains entry to your direct experience and starts rewriting history! If you need more help, Dr. Susan Campbell has created an entertaining game called *Getting Real.*[15] Playing this game with others will help you learn how to tell the truth.

Remembering that you are the source of love (the Second Law of Love) is the key to giving up control. Sometimes you have to be willing to risk losing approval and support if you tell the truth. This is often viewed as risking love. You won't want to take this chance if you're dependent on having someone else's love. In order to speak your truth you need to be free of entanglements! In other words, freedom hinges on knowing that your very nature is pure love.

Freedom and Truth

Some people have the idea that freedom and love are in opposition. In our culture, it is common for men to see love as the enemy of freedom because men are taught that with love comes financial responsibility for a partner, and possibly children. They come to see freedom as power and love as a trap and a burden. Women, too, may fear that love will make them lose their freedom if they have a partner who wants to tell them what to do and when to do it. Love is perceived as a prison to escape, and freedom, is a hard-won prize.

Writer bell hooks beautifully describes the relationship she discovered between freedom and love in her own life.

> *"I looked for love, but I found freedom. And the freedom I found changed my way of thinking about the place of love in a woman's life. I began to see that the proper place for love in a woman's life was not relational love as the source but love generated in the quest for self-realization. By claiming that quest as essential, as the journey that would determine my fate, I realized that the proper place for love was as the solid foundation on which I would invent self and create a life. Uniting the search for love with the quest to be free was the crucial step. Searching for love, I found the path to freedom. Learning how to be free was the first step in learning to know love."*[16]

Many people are tempted at one time or another to sidestep the apparent conflict between love and freedom by bending the truth. The choice seems to be either to lie to yourself about your desire for both freedom and love so that you can sacrifice one for the other, or to lie to your beloved so you won't disappoint them and risk rejection.

The reality is that freedom and love go together perfectly, but only if we are talking about love that is based on truth instead of illusion, and freedom that comes from a total commitment to the truth. When your commitment to what's true is greater than your commitment to your beliefs, or your ego's comfort, or preserving your relationship, you won't hesitate in speaking your truth. Only when your commitment to truth is greater than your commitment to getting your own way, can you offer your beloved the freedom which will inspire love to stay. With this commitment comes both tremendous freedom and unshakeable love.

Another way of saying this is that love and freedom only appear to be in opposition when we forget the Law of Unity. As Osho put it, freedom and love are like the two wings of a bird.[17] Without both wings, the bird cannot soar.

True freedom, like true love, is often mistaken for a false version of freedom. Freedom which honors your autonomy, and your right to self-determination while having compassion for others, is not the same as a pseudo-freedom that makes a point of rebelliously breaking all the rules and abandoning restrictions without regard for anyone else. Freedom without connection generally does not support the pursuit of love.

The belief that freedom and love are mutually exclusive is especially insidious when operating below the level of conscious awareness—as we can see in the following example. Ellen grew up with a father who adored her and provided much support and encouragement for her to be an achiever. He also had very fixed ideas about how she should live her life and what she should achieve. Ellen respected her father and wanted to please him. Her feelings of resentment over his refusal to let her make her own choices as she grew older seemed unreasonable in light of all the help he provided—so she did her best to ignore them. She sacrificed her freedom for what she imagined to be love. She did such a good job of ignoring her resentment over his control that she forgot it was there.

Eventually Ellen married a man who was both supportive and controlling—very much like her father. He was a hard worker, and a good father and provider, but when Ellen tried to pursue her own interests, he balked. Some years later, she came to me perplexed and dismayed by her strong desire to have a secret affair. She didn't dare admit her attraction for another man to her husband because she was afraid he would divorce her. Meanwhile, she found herself increasingly dissatisfied with their lovemaking—while her husband became more and more sexually demanding.

As Ellen became more aware of how difficult it was for her to prioritize her own needs and desires when they didn't match up with her husband's agenda, she realized that it wasn't her husband, but her dependency on her husband's support that was limiting her freedom. She began to see that the sense of helplessness and frustration she felt in her marriage was similar to the suppressed feelings she carried from childhood.

Unwilling to directly confront either her husband or her father with her true feelings, she sought to assert her independence by giving herself to another man. But she was torn between her fear of discovery and her desire to prove to her husband that he couldn't control her. Her unconscious belief that freedom and love were incompatible kept her from seeking solutions based on truth. Once she recognized the real source of her dilemma, she was able to stop pointing the finger of blame at her husband and re-examine her choices.

The Ring of Truth

We all have an innate "truth detector." That is, our bodies know when we are hearing the truth and when we are being lied to. The mind may choose not to be aware of these signals, and can override them to some extent, but the body doesn't lie. This can lead to embarrassing situations. For example, your mind may decide that it's time for some sexual action, but your body is not feeling safe, loving, or turned on and so refuses to cooperate. You may be tempted to see this as a sign of dysfunction or disease, but it's much more likely a healthy message from your body telling you the truth is that sex is not appropriate for you right now.

Some of this ability to discriminate truth from untruth can be explained as the reading of body language such as facial expressions, pupil dilation, body postures, and unconscious gestures. The tone of voice as well as sighs, coughing, and stuttering can also send a different message than the words being spoken. But truth also seems to have a recognizable energy, or vibration, which informs us of its presence, above and beyond these non-verbal cues. This is what is meant by "the ring of truth." If we could measure them, we'd certainly find that the vibration of truth and the vibration of love resonate or amplify each other.

What Is Truth?

One of my favorite definitions of truth is that the truth is that which can not be argued about. I first heard this piece of wisdom from Drs. Gay and Kathlyn Hendricks[18] in a seminar on conscious relationship. At the time I was entangled in a marriage in which there seemed to be no end to arguing, so this statement really got my attention. The Hendrickses teach that untruth encompasses many more forms of communication than outright lies. These include any communication which blames someone else for your own experience as well as superficial or generic responses which avoid personal responsibility.

Another form of untruth would be the false or limiting images we construct of ourselves and others. These are often based on stories we tell to explain why we are stuck in old patterns or excuse ourselves from healing. My friends Art and Ilene came up with the idea of creating a club called *Laughing at Our Stories* or LAOS. To join the club you first have to discover what your core story is. Then you humorously invoke it as an alibi whenever you do something that annoys or upsets your partner.

For example, Ilene traced her lack of self confidence back to an incident where her father criticized her when she was seven years old. Her clingy behavior started to bother Art, and when he complained about it she got even more clingy. This negative spiral was reversed when she began to respond instead by saying, "I can't help it, when I was seven my father called me stupid." Hearing herself say these words reminded her how silly it was for her to allow her life to be shaped by this event. The ridiculous nature of this abuse of the truth, and the joy of putting an end to its power over her, caused both of them to laugh, and a potential argument was defused.

The truth includes bodily sensations, awareness of other events inside your skin such as recurrent thoughts or memories, and direct observation of external stimuli—minus any interpretations you might make. For example, "I notice that you're laughing" is an observation. "You're making fun of me" is an interpretation. Assuming that your interpretations are true is a good way to lie to yourself!

Truth With a Capital "T"

In many spiritual circles, the word *Truth* with a capital "T" is used a little differently from the way I've been using it here. This meaning is more along the lines of the inscription "God is Truth" on the temple in India that Fred Alan Wolf speaks of in his book, *The Eagle's Quest.*[19]

Teachers in the lineage of the Indian mystic Ramana Maharshi often speak of the "Truth of Your Being" or simply "Truth" as a way referring to the Divine, or that which is beyond the human ego. Used in this way, Truth refers to the Absolute Reality which can not be comprehended by the human mind.

The maverick master Osho describes it this way.

> *"I felt a throbbing life all around me, a great vibration—almost like a hurricane, a great storm of light, joy, ecstasy. I was drowning in it. It was so tremendously real that everything else became unreal. The walls of the room became unreal, the house became unreal, my own body became unreal. Everything was unreal because now there was for the first time reality."*[20]

Truth and Reality

We don't always think of truth in this light, but truth and reality are synonymous. When someone refuses to accept reality we call that person crazy. When the discrepancy between what one person sees or hears and the experience of others (consensus reality) is dramatic and obvious, we are quick to apply psychiatric labels. But when it comes to the realm of love, challenging reality is considered quite normal.

We say, "If my husband loved me, he wouldn't criticize me." Or "If my wife loved me, she wouldn't tell me what to do." These kinds of statements are often accepted as true, but if you look more closely, you may find that you can't be sure that they *are* true.[21] They are merely assumptions whose function is to create barriers to love. When beliefs like these are confused with the natural laws of love, we construct a trap which can cause much misery.

We will explore the character of unconditional love in another chapter. For now, let's just say that it's much easier to expect or demand unconditional love than it is to express it. You want your partner to accept you unconditionally, and then you judge him when he doesn't perform according to your wishes. If you were to embody this unconditional love yourself, you would lovingly accept your partner, criticism and all.

A simple test for the truth is: Does it correspond to reality? In other words, you might have the thought, "My husband shouldn't criticize me." It sounds reasonable. After all, no one wants to be criticized. We don't criticize the people we love, do we? Criticizing your partner is no way to create a satisfying relationship, is it? The trouble is that these ideas do not reflect natural laws, they are conditioned beliefs whose origin is the mind.

If the reality is that your husband or wife does criticize you, arguing with this fact doesn't help. The truth is that he *does* criticize you and angrily complaining that he shouldn't, trying to ignore it while silently seething, or haughtily judging him for criticizing you probably won't create a more loving exchange. In fact, according to the Law of Attraction (Chapter Three) all these reactions will tend to exaggerate the hostility between you. What you want is for your partner to stop criticizing you, but the fact is that you can't make your partner change. The truth is that you can only have the possibility to change yourself. If you can change the way you respond to your partner's criticism, you have changed your situation—without requiring anything at all from your partner.

This doesn't mean that you have to allow others to mistreat you in the name of love. When so-called love is used to justify violent and abusive actions, we become confused about what love really is. If you saw violent or abusive dynamics modeled by your parents, and their parents before them, this may seem a natural part of love, but these only masquerade as love.

Purpose and Alignment

Another place where truth and love intersect has to do with the purpose of love and the purpose of relationships. The purpose of love is evolution. We are all familiar with the idea of evolution in a biological or genetic sense, but evolution can also involve spiritual development. Therefore the litmus test for love is always: Does it support the growth and well-being of the beloved?

Love is like a compass, guiding you to those people, places, and actions which are in alignment with your life purpose. Knowing and sharing the truth about yourself with others makes it much easier to find out whether or not you are aligned in this way.

When people have a shared life purpose and similar spiritual values they have a strong basis for relationship. Think of a pyramid where the base is shared purpose, the next level up is common values and perspectives, followed by emotional resonance. Sexual attraction is at the top of the triangle—the icing on the cake. Now turn the triangle upside down and see what happens! Sex too is a compass of sorts, but when it points down instead of up it wobbles!

A relationship based mainly on sexual attraction is often volatile and unstable. It has difficulty encountering too much truth. A relationship created in service of shared purpose thrives on truth. The more truth emerges, the more grounded and vibrant the partners become.

Chapter Six
The Law of Consciousness

Love is the energy of between *that opens to* beyond.
—LEONARD LASKOW, Healing With Love

One of the deepest and most common human fears is the fear of not being loved. Our language encourages us to think of love as a substance, something that can be given, something that can be received, something that can be taken away. We imagine that love is like a pie that can be cut into slices and eaten up. Some slices may be larger and juicier than others and these contain more love. The bigger your piece, the less there is for me. This false image of love as a pie is masterfully laid to rest in a short story by Amy Bloom[22] in which a dying mother explains to her daughter that she interacts differently with each person she loves and that there's plenty of love for everyone.

In reality, love is not an object. We can feel it, but we cannot touch it. We cannot see it, but we can observe its effects. Like oxygen, the presence of love is life enhancing, and has a measurable impact upon the body.[23] Unlike oxygen, love is not an odorless and tasteless gas that can be metabolized and used up. Love is not diminished by its expenditure, but like well-invested capital, the more we use it, the more it grows. If we understand that love is a frequency, a vibration, a state of consciousness, one which can be summoned at will and is totally inexhaustible, our fears of losing love lose their power over us.

This is how one man described his spiritual initiation into Absolute Love:

> *"I felt my heart open to his words. I had not known before that love has a sound, but it was the sound of love that seemed to shatter me. It was like no sound on earth and yet it contained all sound. Nothing could withstand the power of it; every part of my being vibrated, resonating to the sound that revolved and spun out from the center. Everything was sound, spinning and circling, moving the planets in their orbits, permeating every molecule and atom. What I thought I was died in it, was drowned it, was redeemed through it back to the source of life."[24]*

This kind of love is like a radio station, broadcasting twenty-four hours a day. You can always tune in to the love channel. Like a radio broadcast, love is available to an unlimited number of listeners. All that's required is that you find its signal on the dial of your built-in receiver.

Sounds simple, doesn't it? And it is, unless your dial is mislabeled or your antenna has been retracted. If you have grown up confusing love with attachment, dependency, sexual attraction, romantic illusion, lust, infatuation, or obligation you may be tuning to the wrong station. You keep hoping for some really upbeat, feel-good music, and instead you're getting an all-news station. If on the other hand, you haven't learned the arts of trust and surrender, you may have difficulty getting a clear signal. One minute it's sounding great and the next all you have is static.

One of my clients, a woman in her fifties with five grown children, mistakenly believed that "if you love someone, you're supposed to take care of them." After mothering five children, it seemed natural to Sally to take care of her new boyfriend, Jeff, in the same way she'd taken care of her little ones. For several years she offered financial and emotional support, cooked for him, shopped for him, and expected nothing in return except his "love." Jeff was by nature a very emotionally expressive and communicative man. He complimented Sally often and bought her presents. He shared his feelings and was always available to listen when she'd had a hard day. Like her children, Jeff came to rely upon Sally to meet his basic needs. For the first time in her life, Sally felt loved by a man. And she craved this so much she ignored the imbalance she knew existed between them.

When the Jeff became dependent on her support and she became attached to his company, Sally called it love. Jeff began to feel obligated and resentful. When he left her for a woman who didn't care take and "made him feel like a man" she was heartbroken. "I was under his spell for a long time," she lamented. But we could also say that rather than being his victim, she was an unconscious participant in the cultural trance that mystifies attachment and dependency by calling them love.

Actions Speak Louder than Words

I first came to understand that love was a state of consciousness through my association with a small group of very loving individuals who taught more through example than by words. I chose them as my teachers because I noticed that whenever I spent time with them, or spoke with them on the phone, I felt wonderful. I felt accepted, safe, seen, nurtured, understood and free. I felt loved!

My teachers made it clear to me that while I was a special and unique being, they loved me (along with everyone else they loved) simply because they chose to embody love, not because I desired, needed, demanded or deserved their love. The idea of love being a choice was one of many ways their approach to loving differed from what most people believe about love. The thing is, love is a choice you can only make for yourself, not for anyone else. They often reminded me that love couldn't be given or received, only entered. Instead of "falling in love" helplessly or accidentally, they spoke of "rising in love" after removing all resistance.

Eventually I convinced them to publish a short article communicating what they'd gleaned from their journey into love. Here is what they had to say about love as a state of consciousness:

"Love, rather than being a vector, was a space—a limitless space—that any of us could enter by letting go of our protective games. Each one of us had our own door to the room of love, one uniquely shaped in the image and likeness of our naked selves. We had to leave our masks and armor and baggage outside the room of love and could only retrieve them by leaving love. Judgment, taking offense, blame and guilt are a few of the components of that baggage—they exist only outside the room of love.

"We don't need anything or anybody to be in love. But how do we account for that sense of interpersonal love, that caring for one another? We found that when any one of us was in the space of love and when another person, through his or her own relinquishing of ego, entered that room of love, then we were 'in love with each other'—not as a reaction to that person's looks or personality, but simply by ending up in the space of love together. All people in love are in the same space ... From this standpoint, to say 'I love you' means that there is nothing—no personal stuff, distortions, agendas, or needs—in the way of being with you totally."[25]

The Vibration of Love

Have you ever looked into the eyes of a baby who is old enough to focus their gaze and young enough to be innocent of separation, judgment, and blame? This is the vibration of love. Pure, unconditional, natural, no-strings-attached love. There are no words to be exchanged, nothing required other than the willingness to be there and feel what's present. At any moment a sudden movement, sound, or bright light may distract the baby's attention away from you, but it doesn't matter. Once you've tuned to this frequency you *can* take it with you.

Some people find this kind of communion with animals, both domesticated and wild. Others seek it in the presence of a spiritual teacher. One of my most powerful experiences of tuning to the vibration of love came from being with humpback whales.

One day as I was walking across my favorite beach near my home in Marin County, I saw a beached whale lying at the shoreline. When I drew closer it became apparent that the whale was dead. A man and a woman were cutting into the whale's flesh and I soon learned that they were performing an autopsy in order to determine the cause of the whale's death. The United States Navy had been experimenting with low frequency sonar in the area, and some scientists thought there might be connection between these emissions and the increase in marine mammal mortality.

Before all this information could fully sink in, I noticed that a huge wave of sweet energy was sweeping over me. My heart was opening wider and wider, and I felt the strongest sense of being enveloped in love that I'd ever felt. I stood silently communing with this dead whale for many minutes before the stench of rotting flesh overwhelmed me. I silently said a prayer and moved on.

Up to this point I'd had only an average level of interest in whales. Now, I thought to myself, if a dead whale carries such a strong vibration of love, I want to encounter a live one! Luckily for me, my good friend Penelope Smith is an interspecies communication specialist who leads trips to the Dominican Republic where a small number of boats are licensed to take people out to visit with the humpback whales in their Atlantic breeding grounds in the Silver Banks. When I told Penelope about my experience with the dead whale, she offered to take me on her next trip as an assistant.

Some months later, twenty of us braved the rolling and pitching crossing to the Silver Banks, and after resting up and receiving instructions on whale etiquette, we tossed our snorkel gear into small zodiac rafts and set out for the first time to meet some whales. We went out twice a day for the next week, eyes peeled for a "footprint" or a spout which signaled the presence of these gigantic, gentle creatures. We had many marvelous encounters, but the one which made the deepest impression on me was gazing into the eye of a young whale from a distance of about eight feet.

I have no idea how long our eyes met. All I knew was that I'd been left with a sense of complete and absolute love. My mind, my thoughts, past and future expectations, played no part in this at all. In fact, my mind was literally blown. I couldn't remember anything or put together linear time sequences for the rest of the day. I didn't care. I was ecstatic.

Meanwhile Penelope had decided she was going to become a whale. She figured she could swim from port to port with the whales and come ashore occasionally to relay their messages to the humans. She was having a wonderful time fantasizing about what would happen when we returned from the Dominican without her. She imagined people saying, "Where's Penelope? What happened to Penelope?" Then we would all say, "Oh, she decided to stay with the whales. Do you see that skinny white one out there?"

How is it that the whales can open hearts, blow minds, and stimulate such outrageous fantasies? As best I can tell, it's simply the vibration of love. Anyone and anything, living or not, can transmit the vibration of love, but the whales consistently hold this frequency better than any other species on the planet. We humans can only aspire to someday join together in that space of love.

Feeling Unloved

Recently I attended a gathering with spiritual teacher Isaac Shapiro.[26] I love Isaac's gatherings because he is so totally unpretentious. He rarely gives a sermon or a talk, he just responds to whoever shows up.

The invitation extended to any of the fifty people present was to come up and sit beside him and talk about whatever was on your mind. A woman in her mid-forties raised her hand and began to speak about the struggles she was having in relationship, and her fear of being abandoned and alone. As she poured out her heart with a good measure of irony, she suddenly turned toward me and said, "I'm sure Deborah never feels unloved."

I was embarrassed. Apparently this woman knew me from somewhere, but I couldn't remember where I'd encountered her. Most likely she'd attended one of my workshops years ago. Meanwhile, I was sitting there with the certain knowledge of the many times I *have* felt unloved, even when I knew better. In fact, at that very moment, I was overcome with sadness about a recent separation from a man I loved very much.

It's a tricky business, knowing that feeling unloved is a state of mind and one that can change in an instant simply by remembering that love comes from inside. As soon as you come back into resonance with the frequency of love, as soon as you shift your consciousness, you realize love is still there and always will be. But telling yourself that feeling unloved is an illusion does no good at all! You have to make the internal shift. You have to *experience* it. The words mean nothing without the direct experience.

You may still feel grief and be wishing for a different outcome. You may still long to be with your beloved. These feelings of disappointment and resistance to what's so are easily blended with the idea of losing love. Grief and disappointment can be painful, but this pain is small compared to the suffering you create for yourself by imagining that love is gone. As Isaac puts it, "Most of us believe that love is outside ourselves, and someone else is necessary for us to feel love. We do not know where to find love."[27] But this is an illusion. Love is always present and requires nothing from us. We have only to bring our awareness to it.

At the same time, it just makes things worse to compare yourself to others whom you think are more evolved, or to criticize yourself for failing to remember what you really are. Instead of being hard on yourself, see if you can accept yourself unconditionally. It works much better to tune into the vibration of love and meet these lapses of consciousness with the endless compassion and patience which flows from love. Try the practice below if you need help.

EXERCISE:

Totally Lovable Practice: I learned this exercise many years ago from Drs. Gay and Kathlyne Hendricks. I've since shared my own version of it with thousands of people in many different settings. It never fails to generate a strong field of love.

This exercise is best done in a small group of four to six people, but any number will do. One person at a time sits in the center and makes eye contact with the others who are seated in a circle. (If you are doing this alone, look into your own eyes with a mirror.) Each person in the circle focuses their attention on the one in the center and visualizes a ray of light streaming from the center of their chest toward the person in the center. The person in the center maintains eye contact and listens while the others say aloud, "You are totally lovable." This phrase is repeated over and over, using the name (or nickname) of the person in the center. For example, "Janice, you are totally lovable." Meanwhile, Janice does her best to stay present and absorb it all.

After a few minutes, the group becomes silent and just sends the thought, "Janice, you are totally lovable." Then it's Janice's turn to say aloud, "I am totally lovable!" while the group gives her feedback as to whether she sounds like she means it and coaches her to make it more believable if necessary.

When the group agrees that she's got it, it's time for her to look inside and see if there is still something in her that does not feel totally lovable. It might be a body part, a painful area, an emotion, or a judgment. Whatever it is, the invitation is to find the place in the body where this unloveability resides, focus on feeling it, tell the other group members about it, and be willing to receive their healing words, energy, and/or touch to reclaim it back into love. After a brief pause it's the next person's turn in the center.

The Evolution of Consciousness

I have frequently used music as a metaphor for love. Not only do both have a vibration, but the research of Dr. David Hawkins[28] indicates that most music actually does help us tune our consciousness to the frequency of love. Dr. Hawkins has found a way to measure energy fields that are qualities of consciousness. His theory is that humans as a whole are slowly evolving in a more joyful and cooperative direction.

The energy level which he calls love represents a significant shift in consciousness characterized by altruistic rather than selfish motives. It is heart-centered rather than thought-centered. He asserts that when a person has attained this level of consciousness, their presence has the capacity to elevate the consciousness of those around them. This happens effortlessly, without anyone trying to make it happen. In fact, there is nothing you can do to stop it. Not surprisingly, it feels very much like falling in love. This model explains why people benefit from sitting with spiritual teachers, or swimming with whales!

Unlike love as popularly understood, which Hawkins refers to as "addictive sentimentality"[29] this love consciousness increases our intuitive faculties and our capacity for quickly recognizing core issues. According to Dr. Hawkins, when we evolve to this level of consciousness, our brain chemistry changes.

Reliance on linear thought is replaced by an ability to instantaneously perceive an entire gestalt which correlates with a measurable release of endorphins in the brain.

The popularity of various consciousness altering drugs which artificially induce a state of all pervasive love by directly changing brain chemistry shows how much humans love to love. Despite the fact that these substances have unpleasant and detrimental side effects, some people rely upon them as a substitute for the more challenging process of spiritual evolution.

Fortunately for all of us, more people than ever before are exploring a multitude of paths for expanding consciousness. As more and more people make shifting their consciousness to love a priority, they create a context in which it is easier for others to follow. Slowly but surely the consciousness of love is growing.

Chapter Seven
The Law of Forgiveness

To say that one forgives and then not to forget is not to forgive at all. Forgiving and forgetting are part of the same whole. To say that you have forgiven and continue to bring up the problem is a great error and is to carry a large rock in your bowl of light.
—KOKO WILLIS & PALI JAE LEE, Tales of the Night Rainbow

The seventh law of love is the Law of Forgiveness. Forgiveness is both the means by which you can love unconditionally and the evidence of this love. However much you may aspire to express unconditional love at all times and in all circumstances, your human heritage is one of ego-driven conflict and strife.

Our ancestors have not loved themselves perfectly. That is, they have often forgotten that their true identity is love and have instead identified with the personality, emotions, thoughts, or actions. They have judged themselves and even hated themselves. Since self-love is the template for all other love, if you love yourself imperfectly, you will love others imperfectly. You can not love anyone else any better than you love yourself.

The seven laws of love have either not been known or not been honored throughout human history. For the most part, we have loved and been loved conditionally. That is, there are all sorts of strings attached to this pale shadow of love, even if we're not aware of it. You have to earn this so-called love by conforming to a stringent and sometimes mysterious set of expectations. There is little, if any, room for mistakes. As psychiatrist Dr. David Hawkins puts it in his popular book *Power vs. Force*, conditional love tends to be "fragile and fluctuating, waxing and waning with varying conditions. When frustrated, this emotion often reveals an underlying anger and dependency that it had masked."[30]

This Is Your Second Chance

Many have experienced such an absence of anything even resembling love that conditional love would seem to be a blessing. Instead of support, affection, protection and positive regard, they have encountered violence, abuse, disrespect and neglect. It holds true for all of us, but especially if you have a background like this, forgiveness is your second chance.

I recently saw a bumper sticker which read, "Forgiveness is giving up the hope of having a better past." I was excited about this slogan because it hints at the essence of forgiveness. Forgiveness is something that you do for the sake of your own self-love. Letting a person who has harmed or offended you in some way off the hook is beside the point. Clemency for another is much less important than your ability to free yourself from the past and get on with your life.

Forgiveness enables you to stop carrying around a huge weight and come back to the vibration of love. The ancient Hawaiians understood that forgetting is an essential aspect of forgiveness. Each child was taught that he or she was born with a bowl of light and love. Blame, judgment, taking offense—anything that is not love—is like a rock in the bowl of light. Each rock displaces some of the light. Their practice is to check for "rocks" at the end of each day. By simply turning the bowl over, the rocks fall out and once more the bowl is filled with light.[31] This practice is forgiveness. To think about the matter again is to put the rock back in your bowl of light.

Forgiveness cannot be faked or pretended because it is an aspect of love. When you have truly forgiven, you feel as if there is nothing to forgive. You don't need to keep bringing up an incident because you are no longer trying to change or fix anything. You have accepted life as it is. You have reclaimed your original state of love and innocence, and realized that you are stronger than whatever it was that threatened you. If you're not there yet, be honest about it. Find someone who understands the process to help you.

I was disturbed when I first came across the concept that forgiveness also means forgetting. Letting go of my desire for revenge or of guilt about my own failings was one thing. I could see how that would help me. But forgetting the whole thing? My mind went nuts. "If I forget the past, what is to keep me from suffering the same injustices over and over?" I yelped.

Slowly I came to understand that letting go of the past didn't prevent me from doing whatever I needed to do now to take care of myself. The truth is that the more present I am, the more I am able to make healthy choices and the less likely I am to be victimized or to be unkind to others.

It does no good at all to try and deceive yourself into believing there's nothing to forgive. If you are angry, resentful, or ashamed, instead of compassionate and merciful, it's best to acknowledge your true feelings. Holding to a high ideal isn't always the most effective path to love.

Recently a client came to me whose parents had met doing missionary work abroad. In his upbringing there was an emphasis on spiritual values of unconditional love and acceptance. However, anger and hatred were completely unacceptable in his family. As a result, he learned to bury his anger, to hide it deep within his belly, and to express it in covert ways. It took much effort for him to learn to recognize his resentment and call it by its right name, before he could even begin the difficult work of genuine forgiveness.

Whether the inadequacies of your loved ones are major or minor or somewhere in between, forgiveness is the key to releasing their power over you. Some would say that our primary reason for being here is to learn to love unconditionally. Some would say that this is a hopeless task. Forgiveness transforms the intention to love unconditionally from pie-in-the-sky to humanly possible.

It is through your capacity to forgive and forget that you are able to walk the path of unconditional love, with each stumble becoming an opportunity instead of a failure. When your animal nature comes into conflict with the nature of love, forgiveness means reconciliation. Forgiveness is the doorway to unconditional love in part because it allows you to release your conditions one by one, over and over, as many times as you need to do so. If you can forgive and forget, there is always a second chance.

The Habits of a Lifetime

A friend of mine was looking for a special woman with whom to create "a relationship that soars" as he put it. I asked him to describe how he would go about doing this. It all sounded good to me until I heard "zero criticism." Not that I'd object if somehow criticism could be eliminated entirely, but to me it seemed more realistic to acknowledge the deeply-etched grooves of finger-pointing, and practice forgiveness if criticism popped up.

His response was to make a distinction between communicating "there's something wrong with you," versus "there's something I'd like you to look at," or "this doesn't work for me." The first he considered criticism, the next two were not.

The difficulty is that when people are triggered, the distinction may not be made by either the listener, or the talker, or both. Many of us come from generations of finger-pointers. Even if we don't ever want to communicate "there's something wrong with you," in the heat of an argument, it might come out that way. Some people are so sensitive to criticism they might hear "there's something wrong with you" even when what was said was very clearly "this doesn't work for me."

The habits of a lifetime will probably result in speaking, acting, and reacting at times in ways that are less than exemplary—no matter how strong your commitment to embrace the seven laws of love. But if you make it a habit to forgive yourself as well as others, you can take up permanent residence in the space of love.

Evidence of Love

In the documentary film *Fierce Grace*,[32] Ram Dass (aka Dr. Richard Alpert) is reminiscing about his first meeting with Neem Karoli Baba, the Indian saint who became his teacher. He tells us that before meeting his guru there were many things in his past that he didn't want anybody to know. He felt that if people knew everything about him, they wouldn't love him.

The moment they met, Neem Karoli Baba told Ram Dass what Ram Dass had been doing the previous night and what he'd been thinking about. He realized that his teacher had the ability to see everything. As a psychology professor, Ram Dass "knew" this was impossible, but nevertheless it was happening. In an instant he realized that, "Because he knew everything about me, *I was forgiven*. He knew and he loved me."

This encounter toppled Ram Dass's belief system about the unfeasibility of telepathy, or even omniscience, but more importantly it demonstrated the link between truth, love, and forgiveness. This is why people pray to the Divine Mother or Father for mercy. This is why people feel the need to confess their wrongdoings. When someone loves us regardless of our secret "flaws" the separation we feel from love is healed. This healing is forgiveness.

Fellow devotee, Dr. Larry Brillant, makes the following observation: "What staggered me is not that he [Neem Karoli Baba] loved everybody. He was a saint and it's a saint's job to love everybody. But when I was sitting in front of him, *I* loved everybody." Neem Karoli Baba naturally elicited feelings of forgiveness and universal love, even in people who didn't know they had it in them, because he could see this capacity in everyone.

If your idea of love is one of obligation or pretense, you cannot begin to love unconditionally, except perhaps by accident. Encountering a saint or spiritual master can be such an accident. But sustaining this love requires something more.

Faithfulness

When you are newly in love, whether it be with a romantic partner or a teacher, you often glimpse this core of unconditional love, both in yourself and in your beloved. The Austrian mystic, Rudolf Steiner,[33] defines *faithfulness* as the willingness and determination to remember this vision of pure love no matter what happens.

Many people believe that faithfulness has to do with sexual exclusivity. When a beloved fails to honor a commitment to monogamy, it's often difficult to forgive and forget. In fact, this is one of the most frequent reasons for divorce. One alternative is to change your perception of faithfulness. This kind of faithfulness asks that you cultivate your capacity to see the light in the hearts of others even when it's not apparent, even when you've been disillusioned. This kind of faithfulness asks you to forgive and forget.

"Always struggle for the image that you saw," Steiner urges. *This struggle is faithfulness.* Striving thus for faithfulness, we shall be close to one another, as if endowed with the protective powers of angels."[34]

When through faithfulness and forgiveness love becomes more permanent and unwavering, it evolves into joy. This joy is not a response to success or sensory delights. It's simply a natural expression of the love inside. It remains present even when what's happening doesn't look like it will be to your advantage.

From Getting to Giving

Most people believe that love is about getting your needs met or feeling appreciated, valued, and secure. There is nothing wrong with wanting these things; most of us humans want them very much. The mistake we make is in thinking about love in terms of what we will *receive* rather than what we will *give*.

Once you have found love and joy within yourself, it's much easier to love for no reason at all. If you are already full of love, you feel more inclined to let it flow without waiting to see what you will get in return.

My earliest teachers in the realm of love often said that if we would just change our focus from getting to giving, our lives would work much better.

When you're feeling unloved, you may assume that you feel this way because someone has disappointed you or hurt you. Practicing forgiveness may help you let go of your resentment, but underneath it all is still the same old story: I'm feeling unloved, because I'm not getting enough love. If only I could *get* more love I'd feel better.

It sounds reasonable, but as you have probably discovered, trying to get more love usually just leads to feeling needy. Instead, the next time you feel unloved, make it your cue to do something loving or to be of service with no expectation of reward. The popular film, *Pay It Forward,* shows how people's lives can turn around when they shift from getting to giving.

When you are more concerned with what you can give than what you can get, you are far less likely to find fault with your partner for not "meeting your needs." Consequently there are far fewer occasions in which you are called upon to practice forgiveness.

Unconditional Love

Unconditional love is another name for love that is in harmony with natural law. Unconditional love means love with no conditions. It is love without a price tag. Unconditional love expects nothing and demands nothing. It doesn't turn to hate if it's not reciprocated and it doesn't hesitate to see if it's safe to express itself.

Hazrat Inayat Khan put it this way:

> *"It is a feeling that comes only when the heart is tuned to that pitch of love which melts it, which makes it tender, which gives it gentleness, which makes it humble ... It manifests in the love of all, making a man a fountain of love, pouring out over humanity the love that gushes from his heart, and not only to mankind; it may even reach all living beings."*[35]

In the first flush of infatuation, love often seems unconditional but this only because the lovers are blinded to each other's flaws. The fantasy that the beloved is perfect doesn't last beyond the first conflict. From here it is usually just a matter of time before blame, defensiveness, and selfishness creep in.

When I met my most recent beloved, I told him, "You are my perfect mirror. You're the perfect man for me."

Every time he heard the word *perfect,* he would wince, knowing that the appearance of perfection in another has a way of reversing itself. Even though I wasn't saying that he was perfect, only that he was perfect *for me,* this word made him very nervous.

When I speak to people about unconditional love in the context of intimate relationships rather than as an abstract spiritual ideal, the question always arises: Is unconditional love really possible for mere mortals?

Most people doubt that there can be unconditional love between men and women who share a sexual bond. Many feel that it's difficult enough to love unconditionally in less intensely charged situations. Some even wonder if it's appropriate or desirable to love so completely without any reservations. I myself often wonder if it's possible for us to love in any other way.

In the past, mutual dependency, economic constraints, religious beliefs, civil law and societal pressures served to keep marriages intact. These factors have been eroding over the years to the point where fewer and fewer couples decide to stay in unhappy marriages. Now something else is needed to sustain relationships and that something is love. If long term intimate relationships are to survive, love is our evolutionary imperative. Not the Disneyland version of happily-ever-after romantic bliss, but pure, natural, one hundred per cent unconditional love.

The seven natural laws of love can be your blueprint for creating real love in your life. It's not easy, but it is simple. First, you must have the intention. Then, put each law into practice as best you can.

Summary of the Seven Natural Laws of Love

1. Love is its own law. Let love be your guiding principle. When in doubt, listen to your heart. Don't allow mental concepts, beliefs, or assumptions that are not based on love to dictate your behavior.

2. The law of source. You are the source of love. The love inside you is abundant and eternal. You don't need to beg, control, or compromise in order to be loved.

3. The law of attraction. The more you focus on love and gratitude, the more you will be surrounded by love. If you complain, blame, and dwell on fear, you'll attract others who are also resentful, angry, and fearful.

4. The law of unity. Love knows no borders and no boundaries. Love includes everyone and everything. Love takes no position, rising above separation. Find unity within by resolving the conflicts inside yourself and you won't have to act them out with another.

5. The law of truth. Let telling the truth about who you are and what you are feeling and thinking be your foundation. Vulnerable self-disclosure allows for empathy and understanding. The more truth is shared the more love grows.

6. The law of consciousness. Love is a state of consciousness available only when you're willing to relinquish your defenses. Protection is a barrier to love. Love cannot be given or taken but it can be shared. The vibration of love in you is often stimulated when you come into contact with one who carries it.

7. The law of forgiveness. It's ok to make mistakes. Very few humans are able to love perfectly. Forgive yourself and others generously and you'll always have a second chance. Focus more on giving than getting and you'll have much less forgiving to do.

Acknowledgments

I wrote my first book in the year I was blessed to be able to stay at home after the birth of my youngest daughter. Caring for an infant is a heartful and mindless task, perfect for writing during nap times. This time, I had no such luxury and struggled often to keep my mind quiet and clear and my heart open in the midst of many activities. I doubt that I could have done so without the constant encouragement of Celeste Hines who gracefully combined the roles of student, friend, and coach.

I also want to thank all those who have taught me to surrender to love, especially John, Joe, Robert, and Michael. I know it wasn't always easy. I deeply appreciate the mentoring of Joe Dominguez, Jack Painter, Paul Lowe, and Isaac Shapiro. I'm grateful to all of the students and clients who trusted me enough to share their vulnerable hearts, and the friends who believed I had something to give.

Valentine's Day 2005

About the Author

Deborah Taj Anapol has been a relationship coach, speaker, and seminar leader for thirty years. She attended Barnard College, graduated Phi Beta Kappa from the University of California at Berkeley, and earned a Ph.D. in Clinical Psychology from the University of Washington. Her work has been featured on television and radio programs nationwide.

For information on bookings or individual consultations, in person or by phone, e-mail her at lovecoach@lovewithoutlimits.com.

Chapter Notes

Chapter 1: Love Is Its Own Law

1   Hazrat Inayat Khan, *The Sufi Message,* London: Barrie and Rockliff, 1964.

Chapter 2: The Law of Source

2   *Changogya Upanishad* 8.1.2-3 in *The Robe of Love* by Laura Sims, New Paltz, NY: Codhill, 2002.

3   Adyashanti, Oakland, CA Satsang, 2004.

4   *A Course in Miracles,* New York: Foundation for Inner Peace, 1975, p. 11.

Chapter 3: The Law of Attraction

5   Armand and Angelina, *Follow Your Dreams,* Orlando, FL: Heyoka Music, 2003.

6   Riane Eisler, *Sacred Pleasure,* New York: Harper Collins, 1995.

7   In a relationship based on power dynamics, men and women have the same two choices whether or not their relationship is heterosexual. In a same-sex relationship, there will still be one dominant and one submissive.

8   This analysis is based upon the work of Dr. Jack Painter.

9   Masaru Emoto, *The Hidden Messages in Water*, Hillsboro, OR: Beyond Words, 2004, p 78.

10 *Ibid.* p 79.

Chapter 4: The Law of Unity

11 Byron Katie, *The Work on Relationships*, audio tape 2002.

12 *A Course in Miracles*, New York: Foundation for Inner Peace, 1975.

13 *Besieged*, a film by Bernardo Bertolucci, Fine Line Features, 1999.

Chapter 5: The Law of Truth

14 Hazrat Inayat Khan, *The Sufi Message*, London: Barrie and Rockliff, 1964.

15 Susan Campbell, *Saying What's Real*, Novato, CA: New World Library, 2005.

16 bell hooks, *Communion: The Female Search for Love*, New York: Harper Collins, 2002, p.32.

17 Osho, *Love Freedom and Aloneness*, New York: St. Martin's Press, 2001.

18 Gay and Kathlyn Hendricks, *Conscious Loving*, New York: Bantam Books, 1990.

19 Fred Alan Wolf, *The Eagle's Quest,* New York: Summit Books, 1991.

20 Osho, *Autobiography of a Spiritually Incorrect Mystic,* New York: St Martins Press, 2000.

21 Byron Katie is perhaps the most accessible of many teachers who challenge these assumptions. See her website www.thework.org or her book, *Loving What Is* (Three Rivers Press, 2003) for useful tools for harmonizing love and reality.

Chapter 6: The Law of Consciousness

22 Amy Bloom, *Come to Me,* New York: Harper Perennial, 1993.

23 Doc Childre and Howard Martin, *The Heartmath Solution,* New York: Harper Collins, 1999.

24 Reshad Field, *The Last Barrier,* New York: Harper & Row, 1976, p.178.

25 Vicki Robin, "The Possible Relationship" *In Context,* Fall 1984.

26 Isaac Shapiro, *It Happens by Itself,* Haiku, HI: Luechow Press, 2001.

27 *Ibid.,* p 13.

28 David Hawkins, *Power vs. Force,* Carlsbad, CA: Hay House, 1998, p. 90.

29 *Ibid.,* p 90.

Chapter 7: The Law of Forgiveness

30 David Hawkins, *Power vs. Force,* Carlsbad, CA: Hay House, 1998, p. 90.

31   Koko Willis and Pali Jae Lee, *Tales of the Night Rainbow,* Honolulu, HI, 1988.

32   *Ram Dass: Fierce Grace,* A Film by Michey Lemle, New York: Lemle Pictures, 2001.

33   Rudolf Steiner, *Love and Its Meaning in the World,* Hudson, NY: Anthroposophic Press, 1988.

34   *Marin Waldorf School Newsletter,* San Rafael, CA, 1995.

35   Hazrat Inayat Khan, *The Sufi Message,* London: Barrie and Rockliff, 1964.